Aligning the Team with Practice Goals

A How-To Guide for Medical Practices

Susan A. Murphy, MBA, PhD

Maximizing Performance Management Series

Medical Group Management Association
104 Inverness Terrace East
Englewood, CO 80112-5306
877.275.6462

mgma.com

Production Credits
Publisher: Marilee E. Aust
Project Editor: Anne Serrano, MA
Copy Editor: Glacier Publishing
Proofreader: Mary Kay Kozyra
Composition: Virginia Howe
Indexer: Sara Lynn Eastler
Cover Design: Jeff Beene

LIBRARY OF CONGRESS CATALOGING-IN-PUBLICATION DATA

Murphy, Susan, 1947-
  Aligning the team with practice goals : a how-to guide for medical practices / Susan A. Murphy.
    p. ; cm. -- (Maximizing performance management)
  Includes bibliographical references and index.
  Summary: "This book explains how to develop the vision, mission, values, norms, and short- and long-term goals for your medical practice; how to accomplish strategic planning, including the new model of appreciative inquiry. It demonstrates how to set SMART goals and how to strategically link each goal to overall practice goals"--Provided by publisher.
  ISBN 978-1-56829-325-7
1. Medicine--Practice. 2. Strategic planning. I. Medical Group Management Association. II. Title. III. Series.
  [DNLM: 1. Organizational Objectives. 2. Practice Management, Medical--organization & administration. 3. Planning Techniques. W 80 M978a 2009]
  R728.M868 2009
  610.68--dc22
                              2008033010

Item # 7092

ISBN: 978-1-56829-325-7

Printed in the United States of America
10 9 8 7 6 5 4 3 2 1

Acknowledgments

* *

The books in the Maximizing Performance Management Series may have my name on the covers, but they would not exist without the knowledge, enthusiasm, and expertise of many people. Space does not allow me to list everyone, but I want to publicly acknowledge a few colleagues who played especially important roles in the creation of the book you are holding in your hands. Acknowledgments always say "I could not have written this book without their help," but in this case it is absolutely true.

Incentives and compensation are critical components in motivating and rewarding the team, and I turned to two leading experts for help. Laura Jacobs and Mary Witt from the Camden Group contributed this important section. Special thanks go to Steve Valentine, President of the Camden Group, for his enthusiastic support and endorsement of Laura and Mary's participation.

A number of current and former Medical Group Management Association colleagues had special roles in making this series a reality. Marilee Aust understood the importance of this topic during our initial conversation two years ago. Marilee and Anne Serrano, MA are amazing, and the series benefited greatly from their ideas, enthusiasm, and publication skills. I'd also like to thank Julie Sommer, MGMA's talented marketing manager. Drew Di Giovanni and Peg McHugh, formerly with the MGMA, also made important contributions.

Other experts deserve acknowledgment as well for their contributions to different sections of the series. They include: generational guru Claire Raines (the section on generational differences); human resources expert David Milovich (content throughout the series); Matt Mulherin, (success stories as well as the most up-to-date Press Ganey, Inc. research statistics); and Lisa Goddard (editing skills). Real-world case studies make these concepts come alive, and I thank all of those involved including Colleen Conway-Welch, RN, PhD; Deborah W. Royer, MGA; Gene Spiritus, MD; Christy Sandborg, MD; and Bill Zangwill, PhD. Dr. Pat Heim, my mentor and friend for 25 years, generously gave me permission to use information that we developed for our book *In the Company of Women*. Our co-author, Susan Golant, challenges me by example to constantly improve my writing skills.

On the personal front, my husband Jim kept me sane and focused and laughing over the last two years, which was no easy feat. He was my one-man Management Team helping me to maximize my *own* performance while I was writing. I am also blessed with another wonderful support team — my parents, Alice and Bill Applegarth, and my siblings Anne, Ginger, and Paul.

Finally, I am grateful to the thousands of colleagues, clients, friends, and associates with whom I have worked over the years. They have been my best teachers, and I am grateful to now share their real-world lessons with the reader.

Contents

● ●

CD (TOOLS, HELPING MECHANISMS, AND CASE STUDIES)*

Tools/Helping Mechanisms

Americans with Disability Act

Anger

Assess Your Outlook

Benchmarking Your Effectiveness

Checking Your Delegating Skills

Compensation System Self-Assessment Tool: 12 Questions for Better Results

Culture Check Procedure

Decisions by Consensus

Disciplinary Action Steps

Equal Employment Opportunity Laws

Example of Cascading Goals

Exercise: Cash on the Spot

Exercise: External Environment

Exercise: How Are You Communicating the Practice's Mission, Values, and Goals?

Exercise: Name that Mission!

Exercise: Practice Dealing With Minor Errors

Exercise: Purposes Critique

Exercise: The Goal Journey

Exercise: Types of Feedback

Exercise: What Else is Going On?

Exercise: Who Else Needs to Know?

Federal Laws and State and Local Laws

Financial Measures—Which to Use?

Goal Planning Tool

Hiring Employees Checklist

How Good Are You at Performance Management?

How to Give Praise

Integrated Performance Self-Assessment Tool

Key Actions to Align Your Developing Team Members with Goals

New Physician Orientation Checklist

Performance Appraisal Checklist for Managers

Performance Counseling Memo for Discipline

Performance/Feasibility Grid

Questions to be Avoided

Quiz: How Well Does Your Organization Manage Change?

Review Resume in Light of Qualifications Necessary

Sample Balance Sheet Outline

Sample Business Plan Outline

Sample Coaching Plan

Sample Code of Conduct

Sample Code of Conduct for Meetings and Interactions

Sample Conflict/Complaint Resolution Policy (includes Conflict/Complaint Resolution Form)

Sample Conflict Resolution Guidelines

Sample Customer Service Quality Standards

Sample Disciplinary Policies and Procedures

Sample Financial Plan Outline

Sample Medical Practice Satisfaction Survey

Sample Meeting Agenda

Sample Meeting Format Critique

Sample Policy on Workplace Harassment

Sample Strategic Plan Outline

Sample Telephone Standards

Sample Values and Norms

Steps for Terminating a Team Member

What Change Is Occurring?

What Is Your Personal Distress Level?

(continued on next page)

Case Studies

* CD includes CD-only material as well as tools and helping mechanisms from all four books in the *Maximizing Performance Management Series.*

Introduction

• •

As Michael optimistically walks into the Green Valley Medical Group building to report for his first day on the job, he can't help but feel excited. "I've worked so hard to get to this point in my career. I know that I can make a difference in this practice. After all, it used to have the reputation as the best in the city."

It's true that during the interview process, the seven physicians had described a very bleak view of their practice. However, Michael is sure that they were painting an overly negative picture because the last manager had glossed over so many of the problems with patient satisfaction and the staff morale issues, and then to add insult to injury, absconded with $500,000 in cash. Now with the practice on the verge of bankruptcy, the physicians wanted to find a strong manager who would permit them to return to taking care of patients. And Michael knows that he's the right choice. It couldn't be as bad as they represented it. Besides, he's ready for the challenge and has already paid his dues running much smaller practices for the past 15 years.

As Michael steps off the elevator onto the second floor and begins the trek to his new office, he imagines what it's like to be a patient here. Five patients are in the waiting area already, coffee-stained magazines are scattered throughout the room, and two of the patients are talking loudly on cell phones. Michael says "good morning" to the patients as he passes through the private entrance to his new office. Suddenly, Michael is hit by what seems to be a curtain of tension. Karen, the receptionist, has her nose to the computer and grunts at Michael as he greets her with a cheerful "good morning!" Two of the nurses, Ron and Jenna, can't seem to muster any more excitement for Michael's first day either — the two of them appear to be embroiled in their own brawl. "Maybe the physicians weren't exaggerating during my interviews," Michael thought.

"I'll make the rounds and check on the physicians to see how they're doing on my first day here," thought Michael. "They'll probably give me some ideas about where they want me to start." Michael starts with Dr. Samuels, one of the founders of the practice some 20 years ago. As Michael enters her office, he finds her buried under what looks like an explosion of charts, paperwork, personnel files, prescription pads, journal articles, and a plethora of things he can't even decipher. He's reminded of those pictures he's seen on the news of some third-world country after a major disaster has hit — people marshalling any small bit of strength in order to just make it through another day.

After Michael snaps back to the reality that is Dr. Samuels' office, and not a small village after a 9.0 earthquake, his fanciful ideas of riding into a practice on a white horse and cleaning up a few surface-level problems and then basking in the awe of all of his coworkers dies quickly. Michael realizes that he is walking into a workplace that is in need of a major overhaul and that to turn this practice around might be more difficult than building a new practice from scratch. This is no longer a "kick a couple of tires and change the oil" proposition, he has been hired to rebuild the car — but the catch is, he doesn't have the option of buying all of the new parts and just putting it together. He has to decide which parts need the most attention first, take care of them, and then carefully rebuild this machine into a smooth-running, service-oriented, quality organization. And he doesn't have much time.

Throughout the morning, Michael stops by each physician's office, and most of them resemble Dr. Samuels'. As Michael talks to the physicians about their major concerns, many of his first impressions are confirmed by what they say: The office staff is disjointed and unwilling to work with each other. Ron and Jenna just can't seem to get over the different ways in which they communicate — leaving them to pass one another without as much as a glance — and the rest of the staff seems to have joined sides with either Ron or Jenna. More hiring needs to be done, but the physician partners are nervous about hiring any new employees and placing them into this toxic environment. More unhappy employees would make the culture even worse. Patient satisfaction is so low that they have stopped measuring it.

Where should Michael start? It seems like every system in this medical group practice is broken. There is high staff turnover; low morale, low productivity, and low quality; dissatisfied patients; bewildered physicians; and significant financial trouble. Michael decides to begin his journey by taking a systemwide approach that will align team member performance with medical practice goals. By using a systems thinking approach, Michael decides to assess the medical group as a large system with six subsystems that need to be in balance, congruent, and support the medical group's goals.

The subsystems Michael evaluates are from the Weisbord 6 Box model that is discussed in chapter 1. These subsystems include:

➤ Purposes (Vision/Mission/Values/Norms/Goals);

➤ Leadership;

➤ Rewards (and Recognition);

➤ Structure;

➤ Relationships; and

➤ Helping mechanisms.

Each of these subsystems communicates to each team member what is important and how to behave — each subsystem directly impacts patient care. The first step is to define the purposes —the mission, values, and goals — of the medical group. Then Michael must determine which subsystems are not supporting them. Any deficiencies in these subsystems would then be addressed.

On that first day, Michael orders in pizza for the physicians for their lunch break. As he looks at the perplexed faces of his new team of physicians around the conference table, Michael takes a deep breath and officially begins his new job as medical group manager.

Michael begins, "Let's get to work and create a new and improved medical practice. One where you want to practice medicine, your staff wants to work, and your patients want to come for care. Let me start by asking you what you would like your organization to resemble."

"Well," Dr. Black speaks hesitantly, "I just want it to run smoothly."

"But *how exactly* would you like that to look? What are your goals for this practice?" prompts Michael.

"I'll be honest with you," confesses Dr. Samuel, "I don't think I've given it that much thought lately. Isn't that why we hired you?"

"I think it's important that we examine the problems that are affecting your practice currently," reasons Michael. "I know that you physicians are incredibly busy — that's one of the reasons you hired me, but at the end of the day, your names are on that office door. You need to be sure that your staff is a reflection of the type of practice you want to convey to your patients. Rather than mulling over how things haven't gone right, let's focus on the things that are going well in addition to those that need to be rectified so that you can be proud of the practice you've worked so hard to achieve."

Dr. Jordan exclaims, "We agree, Michael. Where do we start?"

Michael explains, "You need to start thinking about what you want your practice to reveal. We're going to rid this practice of its toxicity, and we're going to transform the culture into one that is focused, goal oriented, and people oriented."

Michael spent the next week observing the practice and interviewing every physician and team member about the mission, values, goals, leadership, rewards, structure, relationships, policies, and procedures. After the system assessment, Michael held a strategic planning session for the physicians, senior managers, and stakeholders. After the plan was developed, Michael set out to communicate the objectives to the rest of the staff. The next steps were to align the subsystems with the new goals of the practice.

LEADERSHIP ROLE IN EMPLOYEE ENGAGEMENT AND RETENTION

Michael voraciously researched the recent studies about employee engagement and retention. He was alarmed to read that the Gallup Poll in 2006 found that only 33 percent of the U.S. workforce is actively engaged, while 15 percent of the workforce is actively disengaged at productivity and quality costs of $328 billion per year![1] When leaders were actively engaged, there was a 14 percent higher engagement of employees and 19 percent higher employee retention — highly engaged employees are much less likely to leave organizations within the next year. Additionally, the poll found that engaged employees are likely to be an organization's best source of new ideas. Michael eagerly shared this information with the physician leadership, insisting that they play an active role in engaging and retaining staff.

Michael continued his research and was surprised by the findings from the Center for Creative Leadership® (CCL) about employee engagement and retention. The CCL found that all generations want similar cultures in their workplace:

➤ People want recognition and to feel valued;

➤ Development is the most valued form of recognition, even more so than pay raises and enhanced titles;

➤ Constant learning on and through the job is what people demand; and

➤ Almost everyone wants a coach or mentor, and most want their leaders to serve in this role.

Michael pleaded with the physician leaders to fill these needs for the physicians and team members.[2]

During Michael's meetings with the physician leadership, he cited important research by Press Ganey Associates about the top six priorities for health care employees:

➤ Senior leadership who really listens to employees;

➤ Enough staff to provide quality care;

➤ Promotions to be handled fairly;

➤ Senior leadership who respond promptly to most problems;

➤ Senior leadership who can be trusted to be straightforward and honest; and

➤ Involvement in decision making.

Michael found that attracting and retaining younger physicians was one of the key areas of concern for the more-senior members of the medical staff. Michael provided the physicians with the Cejka Search 2006 Physician Retention Survey that reveals factors such as cultural fit and family as driving forces in physician turnover:

➤ "Poor cultural fit" is the single most frequently mentioned reason for physicians to voluntarily leave a practice (51 percent);

➤ Family is a strong contributor to a physician's decision to leave a practice. Reasons that required the physician to relocate were "to be closer to own or spouse's family" (42 percent); and

➤ The need for flexible schedules, less on-call time, and seeking higher compensation were revealed as factors for physicians leaving practices.

Michael emphasized the critical importance of developing a values-driven, relationship-oriented coaching culture where younger physicians receive mentoring support as they begin their medical careers.

PATIENT SATISFACTION PRIORITIES

Michael has always measured patient satisfaction with the Press Ganey surveys and explained the most recent indices of patient satisfaction to his new medical group. The top six patient priorities include:

➤ Our sensitivity to their needs;

➤ Overall cheerfulness of our practice;

➤ Overall rating of care received during their visit;

➤ Comfort and pleasantness of the exam room;

➤ Waiting time in exam room before being seen by care provider; and

➤ Amount of time the care provider spent with them.

ALIGNING EMPLOYEE PERFORMANCE WITH ORGANIZATIONAL GOALS

Although this book and the Maximizing Performance Management Series as a whole serve as detailed manuals for building a medical group practice for individuals like Michael, *every* organization has systems that can be improved. (Exhibit I-1 shows the flow from individual team member goals to vision, mission, and values, and back again.) So, even though your practice may not be suffering from poor patient satisfaction or enormous staff morale issues or on the brink of bankruptcy, the system-by-system diagnosis and prescriptions in this book and the series will improve the performance of your practice.

The six subsystems as shown in Exhibit I-2 must be in balance in order to align team member performance with goals. Description and exploration of these subsystems appear in the following books in the Maximizing Performance Management Series:

➤ **Box 1: Purposes:** *Aligning the Team with Practice Goals: A How-To Guide for Medical Practices* (Book 1)

➤ **Box 2: Leadership:** *Leading, Coaching, and Mentoring the Team: A How-To Guide for Medical Practices* (Book 2)

EXHIBIT I.1	Aligning Performance with Organizational Goals Triangle

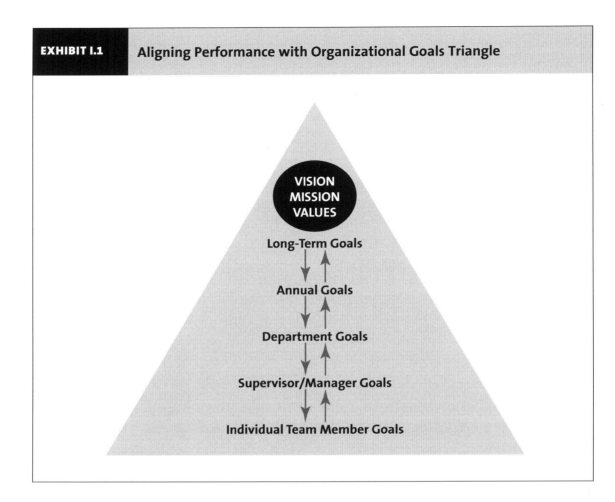

> ➤ **Box 3: Rewards and Box 4: Structures:** *Building and Rewarding Your Team: A How-To Guide for Medical Practices* (Book 3)
>
> ➤ **Box 5: Relationships:** *Relationship Management and the New Workforce: A How-To Guide for Medical Practices* (Book 4)
>
> ➤ **Box 6: Resources/Helping Mechanisms: (CD)** (With all books)

Chapter 1, which is the same in each book in the series, explains the systems approach to aligning team member performance with organizational goals. Every medical practice is a dynamic system with six subsystems. For alignment to occur, each of six subsystems must be in balance and consistently support the medical practice goals. If one or more of these subsystems is weak and is not supporting the medical practice goals, the performance of team members cannot be effectively aligned with the goals. In chapter 1, the six subsystems are explained, and diagnostic exercises clearly define areas of strength and weakness.

A brief synopsis of boxes 1 through 6, including chapter contents of each book in the series, follows.

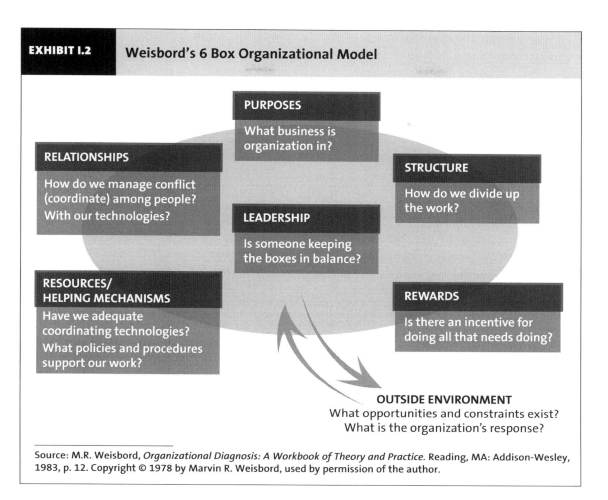

EXHIBIT I.2   **Weisbord's 6 Box Organizational Model**

PURPOSES
What business is organization in?

RELATIONSHIPS
How do we manage conflict (coordinate) among people? With our technologies?

STRUCTURE
How do we divide up the work?

LEADERSHIP
Is someone keeping the boxes in balance?

RESOURCES/ HELPING MECHANISMS
Have we adequate coordinating technologies? What policies and procedures support our work?

REWARDS
Is there an incentive for doing all that needs doing?

OUTSIDE ENVIRONMENT
What opportunities and constraints exist?
What is the organization's response?

Source: M.R. Weisbord, *Organizational Diagnosis: A Workbook of Theory and Practice.* Reading, MA: Addison-Wesley, 1983, p. 12. Copyright © 1978 by Marvin R. Weisbord, used by permission of the author.

BOX 1: Purposes

Aligning the Team with Practice Goals: A How-To Guide for Medical Practices (Book 1)

Chapter 2 explains how to develop the vision, mission, values, norms, and short- and long-term goals for your practice. Chapter 3 explains how to accomplish strategic planning, including the new model of Appreciative Inquiry. Chapter 4 demonstrates how to set SMART goals (specific, measurable, achievable, results-oriented, and time-bound) for each department and how to strategically link each goal to the overall medical practice goals. Next, managers are shown how to cascade the goals developed from the mission throughout the organization and into the individual team member performance plans.

Box 2: Leadership

Leading, Coaching, and Mentoring the Team: A How-To Guide for Medical Practices (Book 2)

The medical practice leadership is crucial for keeping the other subsystems balanced. This section focuses on the roles of the leaders in aligning employee performance with organizational goals. These chapters explore how leaders can effectively "walk the talk" every day and offer several methods for communicating the strategic plan and organizational goals to team members.

Chapter 2 describes the four leadership characteristics that are critical for successful leaders today and the role of emotional intelligence for leaders. Chapter 3 examines the leader's role during change and the fact that although change is inevitable, growth is optional. The four stages for change are described in addition to the leadership actions needed at each stage so that team members can continue to be goal focused despite major changes.

Chapter 4 introduces the Situational Leadership® Model that is a four-stage process for orienting, training, and leading team members by focusing on how well they are aligning their performance with the organization's goals. The four stages are directing, coaching, supporting, and delegating. Through this process, the team member goes from being dependent on the leader for direction in Stage 1 to being more independent in Stage 4, where the leader can both successfully delegate tasks and be assured that the organization goals and objectives are being met. This model ensures that team members know, from their manager, what their goals are and what is expected of them, and then the manager supports the team members as they advance through the development stages in their jobs, culminating in the delegation stage.

Chapter 5 introduces managers to an innovative process whereby a manager can effectively communicate with a team member about his or her inappropriate, non-goal-oriented behavior in a manner that emphasizes both the goals and the performance the manager wants from the team member, and yet does not cause team member defensiveness. This innovative system will effectively address more than 95 percent of team members' inappropriate behaviors and get the team back on track toward goals — it effectively focuses on goals instead of mistakes. Additionally, this innovative system provides a consistent way for managers to discipline team members who are unable or unwilling to align their performance with organizational goals.

Chapter 6 explains how to create a coaching culture where leaders coach the individual team members using a multistep coaching model that includes setting/communicating SMART goals, training team members, building relationships, motivating and using positive reinforcement, monitoring performance, and giving feedback. The goal of the coaching system is to keep both managers and the team focused on aligning performance with organizational goals.

Chapter 7 illustrates how leaders establish a mentoring process for the team, focusing particularly on physician mentoring in both the clinical and academic settings. Young physicians want mentoring and will choose organizations that offer mentoring in order to enhance their skills in the most expeditious way.

BOX 3: Rewards and BOX 4: Structure

Building and Rewarding Your Team: A How-To Guide for Medical Practices (Book 3)

Chapter 2 describes the importance of the rewards and recognition subsystem. It explains the role of compensation and incentives in engaging the team. This important chapter examines what physicians want, how to design an effective compensation system, and how to evaluate your current compensation system's effectiveness.

Chapters 3–6 demonstrate the importance of the structure subsystem. Chapter 3 includes how to interview, select, and hire the most appropriate candidate for the job to be performed. This includes Jim Collins' ideas of getting the right people on the bus and in the right seats. Chapter 4 examines the importance of an excellent team member orientation process, including physician orientation. More than 25 percent of new employees leave within the initial three months; therefore, creating a sound orientation process is critical in aligning employee performance with organizational goals.

Chapter 5 explains the five important components for performance management and how to ensure that each team member's performance aligns with organizational goals. The significant connection between performance management and employee engagement is clarified.

Chapter 6 describes a performance appraisal process that directly measures and aligns team member performance with organizational goals. This chapter discusses the importance of preparation for the performance appraisal meeting through the evaluation to determine the effectiveness of the meeting.

BOX 5: Relationships

Relationship Management and the New Workforce: A How-To Guide for Medical Practices (Book 4)

This book covers the critical subsystem of relationships among the team. Chapters 2, 3, and 4 examine the role of effective conflict management in the medical group practice.

Chapter 2 defines conflict and the cost when it is not managed effectively. Ways to decrease defensiveness are explained and effective conflict management guidelines are proffered to decrease the destructive nature of conflict. Chapter 3 introduces difficult conversation techniques, the difference between content and relationship conflict, as well as the five styles for managing conflict: collaborating, competing, compromising, accommodating, and avoiding.

Chapter 4 includes the role of effective conflict management in team development. The second stage of the team development process, storming, must include healthy conflict or the team development process could be thwarted. Groupthink is discussed, in addition to several types of difficult people who can interfere with aligning team performance with organizational goals.

Chapter 5 introduces gender differences and the importance in organizations of understanding the physiological, genetic, and sociological differences between men and women. These differences are often invisible to us and can cause conflict in organizations because men and women often have differences in how they communicate, make decisions, manage meetings, and view the world.

Chapter 6 introduces generational differences and explains how the four generations in the workplace today have been raised on different planets in many respects. The World War II generation, Baby Boomers, Generation Xers, and Millennials have different viewpoints about leadership, work ethic, teamwork, technology, and many other areas. By understanding the different viewpoints of these generations, leaders can be more effective in maximizing team performance. Chapter 6 reveals the actions that practices can take to attract and retain physicians and other team members of all generations.

BOX 6: Resources/Helping Mechanisms *(CD)*

These files contain many resources and tools, including procedures for managing conflict, guidelines for customer service quality standards, policies for employee discipline, and employment process checklists. Also included are several case studies that demonstrate excellence in efforts to align team performance with organizational goals.

Press Ganey Award winners include practices that have decreased patient waiting time, increased patient education about radiation and chemotherapy, improved patient billing, and enhanced team member satisfaction and sense of ownership.

Vanderbilt University Medical Group, University of California-Irvine Medical Center, and Kaiser Permanente Medical Group in Northern California are highlighted in depth to demonstrate their successful efforts to align team performance with organizational goals.

The bottom line is that this comprehensive, results-oriented book provides a road map and prescriptions to take you and your medical practice to the next level and beyond. Whether you want to fine-tune your practice or manage a complete overhaul of the entire operation, this book provides the answers you need to align the performance of your team with your practice goals.

REFERENCES

[1] The Gallup Organization, "Employee Engagement Index," *The Gallup Management Journal* (October 2006).

[2] R. Plettnix, *Emerging Leader: Implications for Engagement and Retention.* (Brussels, Belgium: Center for Creative Leadership, 2006).

CHAPTER 1

Systems Approach ·····································

Organizations are like humans. Both organizations and humans are systems made up of many subsystems — and each of these subsystems contributes to the overall health of the entity.

What exactly is a system? A system is a collection of things that interact with each other to function as a whole. There are many types of systems: biological, ecological, families, cities, the universe, businesses, governments, hospitals, and medical practices, to name a few.

Experts in health care are now taking a more holistic approach when assessing the health of a person by looking at all the systems in the body. And experts in organizations now look at all the systems in the organization to assess its overall health. This approach is known as systems thinking. Systems thinking is a holistic approach to viewing an organization, to understand how all parts of a system are linked together.

In our human bodies, each organ, bone, muscle, and nerve plays a unique part within the whole body. A strong contribution from one component can't make up for deficiencies in the others.

It's impossible to diagnose the overall health of a person by examining merely one component. Body functions are integrated and their interactions are as important as their individual roles. General practitioner physicians have become the gatekeepers in many medical practices, so all the systems of the whole body can be viewed in a more holistic manner. Specialists are often brought in later to treat individual components that are diseased.

This systems approach to the body can be applied to assessing the health of organizations. The model I like to use in my holistic diagnosis of organizations was developed by Marvin Weisbord and it's called the 6 Box Organizational Model (see Exhibit 1.1). It provides a holistic view of an organization. I think of it as viewing the total system, and its subsystems, from an altitude of 35,000 feet.

The six "boxes" are:

1. Purposes;
2. Leadership;
3. Rewards;
4. Structure;
5. Relationships; and
6. Resources/Helping Mechanisms.

As seen in the diagram, there's a seventh component that complicates these six internal interactions. That seventh component is the external environment. An organization is an "open system," and it cannot be static. As we'll discuss in more detail later, leaders of organizations must be aware of what's occurring externally, that is, outside of their organizations, and these leaders must be proactive. Jack Welch, former chief executive officer (CEO) of General Electric, said, "If the amount of change inside an organization is less than the amount of change outside, then the end is in sight." The rate of change is accelerating and continuously impacts what is occurring inside organizations.

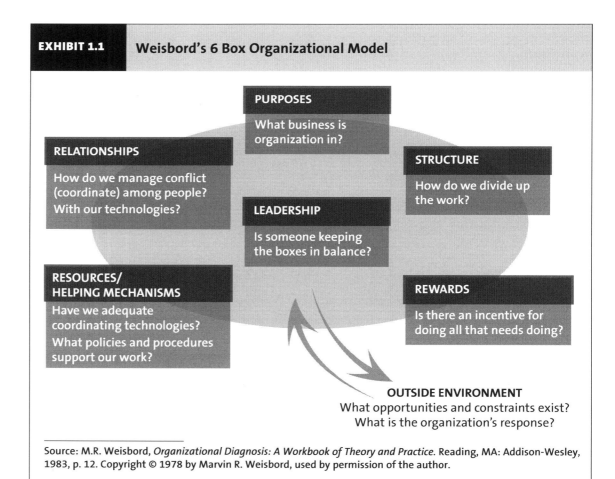

EXHIBIT 1.1   Weisbord's 6 Box Organizational Model

PURPOSES
What business is organization in?

RELATIONSHIPS
How do we manage conflict (coordinate) among people? With our technologies?

STRUCTURE
How do we divide up the work?

LEADERSHIP
Is someone keeping the boxes in balance?

RESOURCES/ HELPING MECHANISMS
Have we adequate coordinating technologies? What policies and procedures support our work?

REWARDS
Is there an incentive for doing all that needs doing?

OUTSIDE ENVIRONMENT
What opportunities and constraints exist?
What is the organization's response?

Source: M.R. Weisbord, *Organizational Diagnosis: A Workbook of Theory and Practice.* Reading, MA: Addison-Wesley, 1983, p. 12. Copyright © 1978 by Marvin R. Weisbord, used by permission of the author.

THIS MODEL WORKS

I've been using the Weisbord 6 Box model to align organizational goals and behavior for 25 years. During the 1980s, I used this model as the organization diagnostic tool for 20 health care facilities when I worked at American Medical International, Inc. (AMI), as an internal consultant. This model can be used in any type of organization. In fact, in my current consulting practice, I've used this model successfully in many industries, including medical and legal practices, hospitals, manufacturing, technology, public relations, research, government, and academia.

In conducting my diagnosis, I analyze the organization using each of the six boxes. I interview managers and team members, asking them questions about the mission and values, leadership, rewards and recognition, structure, relationships, and helping mechanisms throughout the organization.

Several years ago I was part of a "dream team" whose project was to work in a think tank and build the "hospital of the future." This dream team consisted of six individuals — the CEO, four vice presidents, and an organization development consultant (me). Although I started as a consultant on this project, I was fortunate to join the team as a vice president when the medical center opened. We had the prodigious opportunity to build both the physical plant and the organization systems from the beginning. During the two years it took to build the physical structure, we meticulously created the organization building blocks one by one.

We started from scratch — all we had was a big chunk of land in Orange County, California. AMI was bankrolling this project.

We dreamed that our hospital of the future was to be a value-based organization that included systems designed so that everything about the organization — the people, the building lay-out, the medical staff, the volunteers — was aligned to meet our organizational goals. We created an organization based on values and then created systems so that those values were reinforced and communicated throughout every part of the organization, including goal setting, physician recruitment, patient satisfaction, conflict management practices, as well as hiring, rewarding, coaching, promoting, and firing employees.

We used this 6 Box organizational model as the framework for building our hospital of the future. Within the first year of operation, there was immediate quantifiable success. For example, our medical center received several top awards from the corporate office when measured against the other 125 health care centers throughout the United States:

> ➤ #1 in patient satisfaction;
>
> ➤ #1 in physician satisfaction; and
>
> ➤ #1 in employee satisfaction.

There were other signs of success: *Modern Healthcare* magazine named our CEO, John Gaffney, Administrator of the Year. The facility received a full three-year accreditation from the Joint Commission for Accreditation of Health Organizations (JCAHO) during the initial year opening. We had been hoping for one year! JCAHO referred other hospitals to us for help. McGraw-Hill published a book about our hospital of the future: *The Orders of Change: Building Value-Driven Organizations,* written by R.L. Kennedy © 1995.

OVERVIEW OF THE 6 BOX MODEL

Let's examine each of these six boxes, or subsystems, in a generic way by demonstrating the kinds of questions that need consistent answers in order to align team performance with organizational goals. Later in this chapter, I'll elaborate and provide more examples about how to utilize these subsystems in medical practices.

Purposes (Vision/Mission/Values/Norms/Goals)

What "business" are we in? What are we attempting to accomplish? What values should guide our operating processes and are critical to our culture and our success? How are we going to treat each other and our patients?

What are our short-term and long-term goals? Are the purpose, mission, values, and goals aligned so that they are clear and do not contradict one another?

Leadership

Is someone keeping the other boxes in balance? Who is connecting the vision, mission, and values to the strategy, structure, and systems? Who is developing our culture and empowering, enabling, and energizing the team? Who is communicating the purpose, mission, values, and goals? Are all the leaders communicating similar messages through their actions and words? What happens when one of the leaders does not demonstrate that s/he agrees with the purpose, mission, values, and goals? Is there continual coaching and continuous improvement toward the goals?

Rewards

Is there an incentive for doing all that needs to be done? What's in it for the staff to support our purpose? Are we measuring the outcomes that tie directly to our mission and goals? Are we rewarding the values and behaviors that we want? For example, if we say that teamwork is one of our values, are we rewarding only individual accomplishments?

Structure

How do we divide the work? Is staffing adequate? Do we have enough staff members to provide quality work? How many sites do we need in order to achieve our purpose? Are people trained to do the work they are assigned to do so that we can achieve our mission and values? Are the roles and responsibilities clear? Is the workflow design efficient and effective with the most appropriate people performing the job assignments? Does the organizational design prevent duplication of efforts as well as stop assignments from falling through the cracks?

Relationships

How do we manage conflict among people? How do we manage conflict with our technologies? What are relationships like? Is communication open, authentic, and plentiful to align everyone toward the goals? Is teamwork encouraged at all levels? Does the culture of the organization foster trust and collaboration? How are conflicts dealt with among the constituents? For example, in health care, what happens when there are disagreements and conflict among physicians, staff, patients, or families? Is conflict ignored so that it continues to fester and damage relationships, or is it managed openly and professionally in a healthy manner?

Helping Mechanisms (Adequate Resources and Technology)

Do we have adequate equipment and technology to achieve the goals? Is our equipment in good working condition? Do we have policies, procedures, and processes that support achieving our goals? Do we have ample budget to achieve our goals?

Outside Environment External Forces ("Everything Else")

What constraints and demands does the outside environment impose? How are outside forces influencing the organization? How does the global economy help or hinder achieving the mission and goals? Have government regulations affected our ability to achieve the mission? Are unions having an impact on the organization? In the case of health care, what external forces play a role with patients, their ability to pay for services, reimbursement for services from payers like insurance companies and the government? How has the Internet changed patients' access to medical information, and what effect does this have on medical practices? Who are the main competitors? Is there a parent organization that affects the organization?

Subsystems are in dynamic equilibrium. Change in any one subsystem has implications for the others. Every subsystem needs to be reexamined as they shift to ensure that they all still fit. For example, what are the implications if there is a shortage of resources and the income stream declines? What if conflict escalates among team members? What if some leadership members leave?

Careful monitoring of the subsystems is essential for ensuring that there is congruency among the subsystems. No subsystem can operate independently. If one subsystem changes, there will be changes in the others. For example, if there was a change in the relationships box in Exhibit 1.1 — reflecting a change in how conflict is managed among the team members — this change affects all the other internal subsystems and can strain the outside domains as well.

EACH SUBSYSTEM DIRECTLY IMPACTS OTHERS

When constructing the subsystems, it is imperative to understand that each subsystem directly impacts the strength of the other subsystems. For example, if you want to develop a high-performing team approach, it is critical that all six boxes facilitate and foster team behavior. The leaders would commit to work as a team, model team behavior, and train others how to behave on a high-performing team. The mission statement and values would include teamwork. The reward and recognition system would reward team-building behaviors and provide discipline for selfish, solitary ones. The team member relationships would receive a lot of focus, and members would be taught conflict management techniques and communication and collaboration skills. The organization structure would discourage "silos" and foster teamwork. The mechanisms would include state-of-the-art equipment in good working condition in order to facilitate productive effort and working relationships.

COMMUNICATING TO TEAM MEMBERS

It's through the six subsystems — purposes, leadership, rewards, structure, relationships, and mechanisms — that team members learn what is important and how they should perform. The leaders are responsible for ensuring that the messages the team receives are consistent and clear, and that they are focused on the customer as well as the vision, mission, and values. See Exhibit 1.2 for examples of the communications that come through loud and clear to team members.

EXHIBIT 1.2	Communications that Come through Loud and Clear to Team Members

Reward systems	The way people dress
Verbal language	Style of leadership
Body language	Letters to customers
Office layouts	Formal communication
Working conditions	Informal communication
Decision-making process	Website
Human resources policies	E-mails from leadership
Benefits	Treatment of customers
Professionalism of leaders	Respect displayed
Cues	Organizational structure
Process improvement systems	Work distribution
Working relationships	Conflict management
Signals and codes that come from leadership actions	Training/Development opportunities
Types of feedback given — coaching/disciplining	Where budget is spent
Promotions	Value hiring
Demotions	Values
Coaching, mentoring	Celebrations
On-boarding process	Press releases to community
Actions by leaders	

© 2009 Susan A. Murphy, MBA, PhD

CREATING AN ALIGNED AND CONGRUENT ORGANIZATION, ONE SUBSYSTEM AT A TIME

Asking the question "If it were perfect, what would this subsystem look like?" can be a very effective process for creating an aligned and congruent system. For example, If it were perfect, what would our mission be? If it were perfect, what would our leadership look like? What about our reward and recognition system? Our structure? Our relationships and how we manage conflict? Our helping mechanisms?

Throughout the chapters in this book, we'll be examining each of the subsystems, and we'll see that by strengthening each of the six boxes, we can strengthen the overall medical practice. See Exhibit 1.3 for the 6 box model in input/output terms.

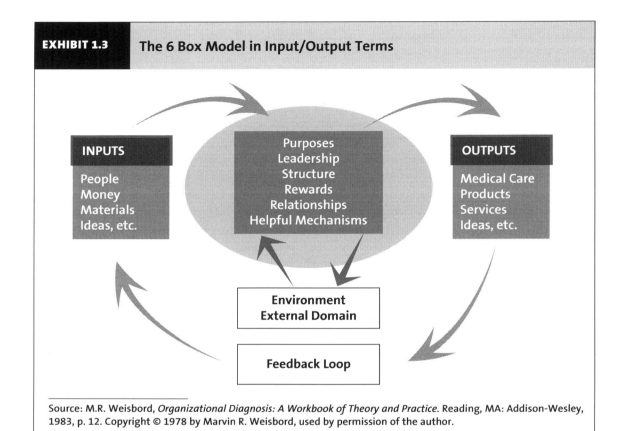

EXHIBIT 1.3   **The 6 Box Model in Input/Output Terms**

INPUTS

People
Money
Materials
Ideas, etc.

Purposes
Leadership
Structure
Rewards
Relationships
Helpful Mechanisms

OUTPUTS

Medical Care
Products
Services
Ideas, etc.

Environment
External Domain

Feedback Loop

Source: M.R. Weisbord, *Organizational Diagnosis: A Workbook of Theory and Practice.* Reading, MA: Addison-Wesley, 1983, p. 12. Copyright © 1978 by Marvin R. Weisbord, used by permission of the author.

DIAGNOSING POTENTIAL EXTERNAL DISRUPTIONS

Another way to think about the six boxes is that each is continually being juggled to keep up with shifting — and uncertain — winds in the external domain, or as "everything else outside." These external domains include the following:

➤ Customers (patients, families, visitors);

➤ Suppliers (of materials, pharmaceuticals, capital, equipment, space);

➤ Competitors (for both markets and resources);

➤ Regulatory groups (government, unions, trade associations, certifying groups); and

➤ Parent organizations (university, central headquarters, corporate office).

So, as we're building and strengthening a medical practice, it helps to discover how the external domain is straining the internal subsystems (relationships, rewards, leadership, structure, etc.) as well as how the internal issues may be straining relations with one or more important external domains. See Exhibit 1.4 for a diagnostic tool to benchmark your team effectiveness.

EXHIBIT 1.4	Benchmarking Your Team Effectiveness

20 CHARACTERISTICS OF HIGH-PERFORMING TEAMS

The 20 characteristics in this diagnostic tool are based on characteristics of high-performing teams. Distribute this questionnaire among your team members and have them complete it anonymously. The characteristics are in the Likert scale format to be scored 1 to 7, where 1 means this characteristic in not present in your team and 7 means it is very evident.

Collect the instrument from your team members and for each of the characteristics, calculate the mean score and the range. This will demonstrate where your organization is excelling and where you can focus on continuous improvement to increase your team's performance. The lower the mean score and the wider the range, the more attention the characteristic requires from you as the leader. The optimum scores are a high mean and narrow range.

INSTRUCTIONS FOR EXERCISE

Indicate your assessment of your team and the way it functions by circling the corresponding number on a scale of 1 (low) to 7 (high).

Choose the number that you feel is most descriptive of your team.

1. MISSION/VISION/GOALS/PRIORITIES

(Low)　Team members don't know the mission/vision/goals/priorities.

(High)　Team members completely understand and agree with mission/vision/goals/priorities.

1　　2　　3　　4　　5　　6　　7

2. VALUES AND STANDARDS

(Low)　We have very different values, and our standards are not clear.

(High)　We all understand our values and standards and strive constantly to live up to them.

1　　2　　3　　4　　5　　6　　7

3. BRANDING

(Low)　We are not different from similar organizations; our reputation is not distinguishable.

(High)　Our brand is clear. Patients come to us because we're the best.

1　　2　　3　　4　　5　　6　　7

4. LEADERSHIP

(Low)　One person dominates, and leadership roles are not shared.

(High)　There is full participation in leadership; leadership roles are shared by members.

1　　2　　3　　4　　5　　6　　7

(continued)

EXHIBIT 1.4 *(continued)*	**Benchmarking Your Team Effectiveness**

5. EMOTIONAL INTELLIGENCE

(Low)   Leaders do not practice self-management, self-control, or empathy.

(High) Leaders practice self-management, self-control, and empathy.

1   2   3   4   5   6   7

6. LEADERSHIP COMMUNICATION

(Low)   We do not know what is going on in other parts of the organization.

(High) We are informed about important issues within the organization.

1   2   3   4   5   6   7

7. STRUCTURE

(Low)   Our organizational structure is neither efficient nor effective.

(High) Our organizational structure is efficient and effective.

1   2   3   4   5   6   7

8. TRAINED, PROFESSIONAL TEAM

(Low)   Staff is not oriented nor trained in their jobs.

(High) Staff is oriented, well trained, and professional.

1   2   3   4   5   6   7

9. PERFORMANCE

(Low)   We can't get projects finished; we don't follow through on commitments.

(High) We deliver on time, on budget, and follow through on commitments.

1   2   3   4   5   6   7

10. UTILIZATION OF RESOURCES

(Low)   Member resources are not recognized or used.

(High) Member resources are fully recognized and used.

1   2   3   4   5   6   7

11. ROLES AND RESPONSIBILITIES

(Low)   Team members are unclear in their roles, responsibilities, and performance expectations.

(High) There is clarity in job roles and responsibilities of team members.

1   2   3   4   5   6   7

12. REWARDS AND RECOGNITION

(Low)   Outstanding performance is neither recognized nor rewarded.

(High) Outstanding performance is always recognized and rewarded.

1   2   3   4   5   6   7

13. TRUST AND CONFLICT

(Low)   There is little trust among members, and conflict is evident.

(High) There is a high degree of trust among members. Conflict is dealt with openly and worked through.

1   2   3   4   5   6   7

14. COMMUNICATION/LISTENING

(Low) We are guarded and cautious in team discussions, and we don't listen to each other.

(High) We are open and authentic in team discussions, and we listen and feel understood.

| 1 | 2 | 3 | 4 | 5 | 6 | 7 |

15. DEGREE OF MUTUAL SUPPORT

(Low) We operate on the basis of everyone for himself/herself.

(High) We show genuine concern for each other.

| 1 | 2 | 3 | 4 | 5 | 6 | 7 |

16. DIVERSITY

(Low) Prejudice exists among team members and differences are not appreciated or respected.

(High) Differences among team members are respected and appreciated.

| 1 | 2 | 3 | 4 | 5 | 6 | 7 |

17. PROBLEM SOLVING/DECISION MAKING

(Low) There is no consistent way that problems are solved or decisions are made.

(High) Team has well-established and agreed-upon approaches to problem solving and decision making.

| 1 | 2 | 3 | 4 | 5 | 6 | 7 |

18. CONTROL AND PROCEDURES

(Low) There is little control and a lack of procedures to guide team functioning.

(High) There are effective procedures; team members support these procedures and regulate themselves.

| 1 | 2 | 3 | 4 | 5 | 6 | 7 |

19. INNOVATION/CHANGE/CREATIVITY

(Low) The team is rigid and does not experiment with how things are done.

(High) The team experiments with different ways of doing things and tries new ideas.

| 1 | 2 | 3 | 4 | 5 | 6 | 7 |

20. CELEBRATION

(Low) Successes are not acknowledged or celebrated.

(High) Team acknowledges and celebrates successes.

| 1 | 2 | 3 | 4 | 5 | 6 | 7 |

Exercise   **What Else Is Going On? Scanning "Everything Else"**

How satisfactory do you view current transactions between these external domains and your medical practice?

	Highly Unsatisfactory				Highly Satisfactory
Patient/Family/Visitor	1	2	3	4	5
Supplier	1	2	3	4	5
Competitor	1	2	3	4	5
Regulator	1	2	3	4	5
Parent organization	1	2	3	4	5

Do you have any influence over the situation?

_____

_____

NOTE: This exercise is also on the CD.

Exercise   **External Environment**

List three important environmental demands that influence your practice's strategic mission (major purpose for existing).

1. _____

2. _____

3. _____

NOTE: This exercise is also on the CD.

CHAPTER PRESCRIPTIONS

➤ Ensure that the leaders in your organization are aware of what's occurring externally (outside the organization) and become proactive leaders.

➤ Increase awareness by the managers as well as the team members about the subsystems and together work toward fulfilling the mission and values, leadership, rewards and recognition, structure, relationships, and helping mechanisms throughout the organization.

➤ Understand that each subsystem does not work independently of the other, but rather directly impacts the strength of the others.

CHAPTER 2

Developing the
Organization's Purpose......................

Asking the question "If it were perfect, what would this subsystem look like?" can be a very effective process for creating an aligned and congruent system. So, if it were perfect, what would the purpose be?

BOX 1: PURPOSES — VISION/MISSION/VALUES/NORMS/SHORT- AND LONG-TERM GOALS

Developing the vision, mission, values, norms, and short- and long-term goals is a critical step in building an aligned organization. Without a clear purpose and direction, team members become confused, unproductive, and less motivated.

Two decades ago, I had the privilege of hearing Dr. Peter Senge describe visionary leadership. He drew three pictures (originated by David Peter Stroh) on a flip chart. The first picture (Exhibit 2.1) depicted a simple organization where each arrow represents a person.

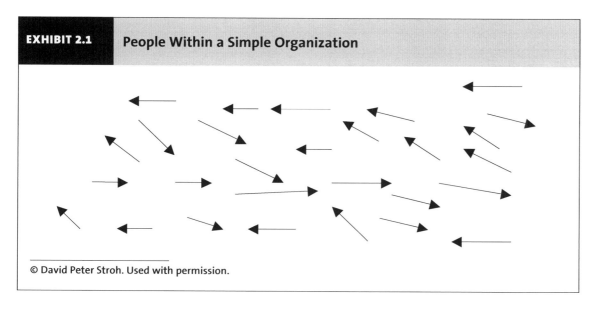

EXHIBIT 2.1 | **People Within a Simple Organization**

© David Peter Stroh. Used with permission.

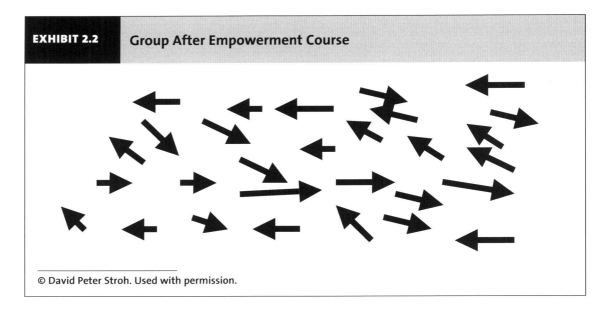

EXHIBIT 2.2   Group After Empowerment Course

© David Peter Stroh. Used with permission.

Exhibit 2.2 demonstrates what happens when the manager sends the group to an empowerment course so they develop more energy and excitement about a project. The people become stronger and more determined, albeit going in different directions.

Exhibit 2.3 illustrates how people will energetically align themselves as they move toward achieving a shared vision, mission, values, and norms.

Looking down from 35,000 feet in the air, let's focus on the subsystems directly related to aligning the team's performance to organizational goals.

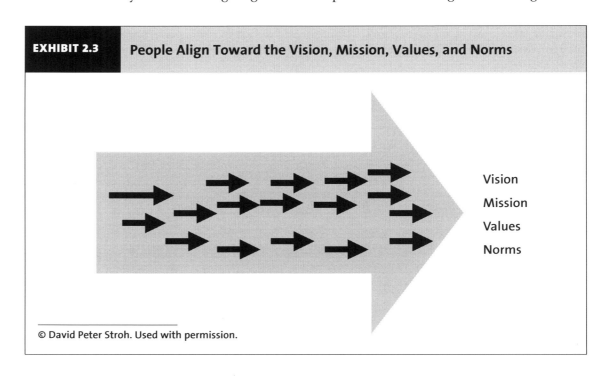

EXHIBIT 2.3   People Align Toward the Vision, Mission, Values, and Norms

Vision

Mission

Values

Norms

© David Peter Stroh. Used with permission.

Box 1 — the purposes and goals box — is where you want to be in the future. There are two categories of goals: broad (not measured) and specific (measured). The broad goals include the vision, mission, values, and norms. The specific goals include long-term and short-term goals. These goals set the organization's direction.

Box 1 provides staff members in organizations with a shared vision, mission, and values, aligning their energies in one direction, therefore reducing conflict and harnessing everyone's energies toward the same end. Without shared focus and direction, people work at cross-purposes and act according to their individual inclinations. Without direction, the organization lacks purpose, and team members become ineffective, nonproductive, and confused as to where they are going. There are several components to Box 1 (see Exhibit 2.4), and each must relate easily to the others:

➤ The vision, as a goal, is a picture of what we want to look like in the future.

➤ The mission, as a goal, describes why we exist. What do we contribute to society? At all levels, the mission answers the following questions: "Why do we exist? What do we contribute to the organization?"

➤ Values, as goals, are what we preach, what we believe to be true, and what we stand for. Values have spiritual overtones.

➤ Norms, as goals, are the rules of conduct. They reflect how we behave and how we are observable. The mission and values give direction, whereas the norms give boundaries. The norms should be in sync with our values.

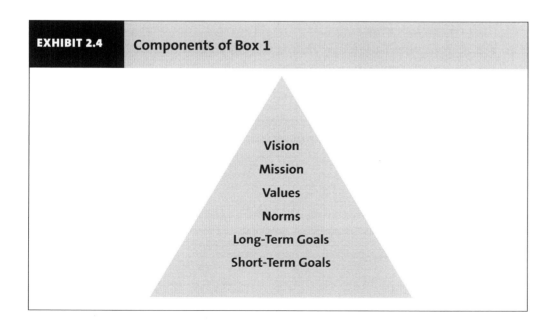

EXHIBIT 2.4   Components of Box 1

Vision

Mission

Values

Norms

Long-Term Goals

Short-Term Goals

THE VISION FOR THE FUTURE

Let's first look at vision and mission. Developing a vision and mission injects a sense of purpose into the organization's activities. These tools provide long-term direction and give the firm a strong identity. In creating the vision and mission, you are collectively deciding who you are, what you are here for, what you believe in, what you want to be known for, and where you are headed.

The vision is a picture of where you want to be some time in the future.

Some visions from well-known people include:

➤ Martin Luther King: "I have a dream" — describes his vision for a non-racist America.

➤ President John F. Kennedy: "By the end of the decade, we will put a man on the moon."

➤ American Red Cross Chapter: "To be recognized as a compassionate organization setting the standard for alleviating human suffering."

➤ Walt Disney: "To Be the Happiest Place on Earth." There's a legend that goes with Disney's vision. Disney had died by the time Disney World opened. As the story goes, there was a private celebration for corporate executives at the park in Orlando, Fla., on opening day. During the festivities, one of the managers approached Mrs. Disney and told her that his only bad feeling that day was remorse that Disney did not live to see his creation. Her response was, "You fool! Of course he saw it. How do you think it got here?"

Another legend about visions concerns a couple touring an eastern European city where they came upon an immense construction site. At this stage the project was little more than a hollow opening in the ground, and the curious couple asked one crew member, "Excuse us, but this is a very impressive project. What are you doing here?" The abrupt and almost rude answer from the man who appeared to be in charge was, "We're digging a hole!" Not satisfied by that smug response, they asked the same question. This time the response was, "We're digging a foundation." Still lacking the information they hoped to get, they repeated the question to the third worker. This time they heard, "We're building a cathedral." So, is your team digging a hole or building a cathedral? If digging a hole, what have you done to allow them to have such a limited view of their roles? How might you expand their view to include worthwhile and important work?

In creating your vision, it's important to aim high because you will never be greater than the vision that guides you! The vision is a statement about what the future of the organization will look like.

Some of the characteristics of a good vision include:

- ➤ Creates a mental picture of a future state (what success looks like);

- ➤ Focuses on "what" we do vs. "how" we do it;

- ➤ Engages our heart and our spirits, and captures imagination;

- ➤ By definition is "cloudy and grand" (If clear, it would not be a vision.);

- ➤ Answers "Where are we going? Who/What will we be when we get there?";

- ➤ Provides meaning for the work people do;

- ➤ Is a living document that can always be added to; and

- ➤ Should challenge and inspire the group to achieve its mission.

Vision provides physicians and team members with an image of an ideal future state that is sensible and practical on the one hand, but emotionally uplifting and compelling on the other. Jack Welch, former chief executive officer of General Electric, said, "Good business leaders create a vision, articulate the vision, passionately own the vision, and relentlessly drive it to completion."

STRUCTURAL TENSION

Dr. Peter Senge, bestselling author of *The Fifth Discipline*,[1] taught me about the "structural tension" that occurs when you think about your vision (of where you want to be) and your current reality. The farther your vision is from your current reality, the higher the tension level — and the greater the discomfort. To decrease this structural tension, you can either move your current reality (your current state) toward your vision or lower your vision (your goals) to be closer to your current reality. We often will lower our goals because that's easier. I recommend that you keep your vision high and fight the temptation to lower your vision when the going gets tough. You will never be greater than the vision that guides you.

THE MISSION OF MISSIONS

The mission statement clarifies the purpose of the organization, why it exists, what the organization is seeking to do, and what it is trying to accomplish for its customers. Missions tend to be stable over time. Some characteristics of a useful mission include:

- ➤ Brief and sharply focused;

- ➤ Clear, understood by everyone;

- ➤ Specific — tells why you do what you do, why you exist (patient care, provide jobs to the community, maximize shareholder value);

- ➤ Actionable — you can use it to make decisions, provides direction for doing the right things;

- Inspires commitment;
- Does not prescribe means;
- Sufficiently broad;
- Addresses our opportunities;
- Serves as the credo of the leaders;
- Says what, in the end, we want to be remembered for; and
- Involves daily decisions that should reflect the mission/vision.

Mission statements can fail if they:

- Use fuzzy, nonspecific language;
- Include interchangeable goals or visions that can be adopted by any company when only a few words are changed;
- Lack true, prolonged leadership support — in action more than in words; and
- Are poorly implemented.

Mission Statements

Following are three examples of mission statements:

> *Vanderbilt University Medical Center's mission is to bring the full measure of human knowledge, talent, and compassion to bear on the healing of the sickness and injury and the advancement of health and wellness through preeminent programs in patient care, education, and research.*

> *At Kaiser Permanente, our mission is to provide affordable, high-quality health care services and improve the health of our members and the communities we serve.*

> *Our mission is to serve the community with excellent, timely, and compassionate patient care, empowering people toward wellness in body, mind, and spirit.*

My own mission is "to serve as a catalyst in the optimum development and performance of people and their organizations." Values are beliefs the organization members hold in common and endeavor to put into practice.

THE VALUE OF VALUES

Values guide the organization members in performing their work. Values answer the question: "What are the basic beliefs that we share as an organization?" Strong values statements keep an organization on track. They help foster the right choices in both day-to-day and strategic decision making. Along with mission and vision, they provide the board, physicians, and team members a foundation for addressing new challenges, including financial crises and strategies to cope with changes in the environment. They help with tricky ethical questions that stray into gray areas. In periods of turbulent change, values provide stability.

Developing meaningful values can be an important investment in an organization because strong values provide the foundation for the culture and can positively affect the recruitment, retention, and commitment of staff and patients. Leaders must know what they care about, because you can only be authentic when leading others according to the principles that matter most to you. Otherwise, you're just putting on an act. Plus, if the leader's values are not the same as the organization's, it is impossible to align performance with goals. Leaders who want to clarify their own values can ask themselves questions such as:[2]

- What do I stand for? Why?
- What do I believe in? Why?
- What causes me discontent? Why?
- What keeps me awake at night? Why?
- What am I passionate about? Why?
- What brings me suffering? Why?
- What makes me jump for joy? Why?
- Just what is it I really care about? Why?

Researchers have found that there are three central themes in the values of highly successful, strong-culture organizations:[3]

- High performance standards;
- A caring attitude toward people; and
- A sense of uniqueness and pride.

I've done consulting work in several divisions of Johnson & Johnson (J&J), and whenever I sign a contract with a different division, I'm asked, "Have you read our credo?" From my experience with J&J, I've found that the credo is a fundamental part of the values of every J&J employee whom I've met. Students for decades have held class discussions about J&J's decision to remove Tylenol® from store shelves after finding that some were laced with poison. Although at the time it was expensive to destroy all that Tylenol®, their credo dictated that destroying the Tylenol® supply before another death occurred was the best action. Although J&J lost money one year because of that decision, by being true to their credo, employees, consumers, and Wall Street have remained loyal to them.

Some examples of values for medical practices include:

- Commitment to excellent services;
- Innovation;
- Diversity;
- Creativity;
- Honesty;
- Integrity;
- Teamwork;
- Trust;
- Accountability; and
- Continuous improvement.

As another example, the Vanderbilt University Medical Center and Medical Group's credo states their values:

- Service to our patients and our communities;
- Education and research;
- Respect for our patients and for each other;
- Quality, efficiency, and cost effectiveness;
- Collaboration and caring; and
- Careful use of our resources.

MEDICAL GROUP MANAGEMENT ASSOCIATION

Last year I was presenting this information about vision, mission, and values to Dr. Bill Jessee and his senior management team of MGMA in Englewood, Colorado. As Dr. Jessee listened intently to the rationale behind the Box 1 elements, he quickly understood the benefits to an organization of having clear vision, mission, and values. MGMA at that time had several different statements. Under Dr. Jessee's guidance, MGMA now has one clear mission, vision, and set of values.

MGMA's Mission, Vision, and Values

Mission: To continually improve the performance of medical group practice professionals and the organizations they represent.

Vision: To be the recognized leader in defining and supporting the profession of medical group practice management.

Values: Our values drive everything we do. We believe in:

- Patient-focused care;
- Group practice as the optimal framework for quality patient care;
- Setting standards for professional performance;
- Continuous learning for professional growth;
- Evidence-based clinical and managerial decision making;
- Physician and administrator teamwork;
- Inclusiveness and diversity;
- Service to community and the profession; and
- Integrity, collegiality, and respect for the individual.

NORMS FLOW FROM THE VALUES

After developing meaningful values, the next step is to develop norms to go with the values. The norms are the behaviors that demonstrate the values. I sometimes call these rules of conduct or codes of conduct. Some successful organizations make these rules of conduct a part of the performance appraisal system and evaluate all team members by the same code. At our "hospital of the future," 50 percent of every performance appraisal was based on how well the team member lived the values and norms on a day-to-day basis. Exhibit 2.5 is a sample of values and norms. Exhibit 2.6 shows more descriptive norms.

Exhibits 2.7 and 2.8 show samples of codes of conduct. For a sample credo, look a the Vanderbilt case study on the accompanying CD.

EXHIBIT 2.5   Sample Values and Norms

OUR VALUES AND NORMS

TEAMWORK — Accomplishing our goals through a collaborative focus.

Recognizes and demonstrates the worth and importance of others, preserving the emotional and spiritual dignity, confidentiality, and privacy of all external and internal customers.

ETHICAL STANDARDS — Doing the right thing to ensure compliance.

Conducts himself/herself in an honest, fair, and straightforward manner.

QUALITY — Doing the right things consistently, correctly, and safely as they relate to all interactions provided by every team member.

1. Applies performance improvement principles and processes in individual and group activities to develop organizational systems and structures.

2. Uses resources (supplies, labor, and equipment utilities) in a cost-effective manner to remain within budget.

ACCOUNTABILITY — Taking responsibility for your own actions, both on a personal and professional basis.

1. Takes ownership of daily activities, processes, and outcomes.

2. Aligns behaviors of conduct and safety with organizational policies and mission.

3. Adheres to attendance standards.

4. Adheres to customer service House Rules.

INTEGRITY — Committing to personal respect, honesty, and ethical actions in all situations.

Conducts himself/herself in an honest, fair, and straightforward manner.

DEDICATION — Consistently demonstrating a belief that teamwork involvement and follow-through are essential and used in all endeavors.

1. Responds to the feelings and emotional needs of all customers in gentle and caring ways.

2. Meets the individualized needs of our customers in a sensitive manner, including recognition of cultural diversity.

3. Meets commitments to all customers in a consistent, positive, and timely manner.

Customers are patients, visitors, doctors, vendors, and all team members.

EXHIBIT 2.6 **Sample Values and Norms — More Descriptive Norms**

OUR VALUES AND NORMS

Ethical: Our conduct is exemplified by honesty and integrity. This applies in all relationships (business and personal), internally and externally.

Respectful: We will communicate/interact with fellow team members, patients and families, visitors, and vendors as we would want them to communicate/interact with us.

Teamwork: We are players on a single team. We must work in unity to achieve our mission. We will develop and maintain strong internal relationships through open and constructive communication. We are expected to be part of the solution, not part of the problem.

Commitment/Dedication: We demonstrate commitment and dedication by doing our best and going the extra mile to get the job done. All team members have the responsibility to live up to the commitments we make in a timely manner, and to make every effort to present useful and accurate information in a professional way.

Proactive/Empowerment: Our behavior and actions should reflect a commitment to timeliness and a sense of urgency — in dealing with patients, families, and other team members. This approach optimizes mutual efficiency and ensures that we make the most of our opportunities. We should also make decisions and proactively develop strategies designed to achieve our mission.

Professional: We shall be professional in all of our interactions, including our attire, appearance, conduct, and communications.

Fiscal Responsibility: We can only stay in business — and continue to service our patients — as long as we are profitable. Profitability requires fiscal responsibility. Each team member impacts our profitability and growth. We all have a shared responsibility to develop strategies, capitalize on opportunities, and use our resources wisely and efficiently.

Positive Environment: We are committed to maintaining an environment that breeds success. We believe in an atmosphere that encourages unity, innovation, and freedom to create. We celebrate, reward, and recognize one another when goals are met. We all must do our part to contribute to an enthusiastic, collegial, vibrant, and productive environment.

Strive to Exceed Expectations: All of us have the independent obligation to strive to exceed our patients' expectations. Our patients' positive perspective of their relationship with us is the key to our success. Every patient interaction has a definite impact on the success or failure of our commitment. Therefore, each team member has total authority and, with it, the obligation to make every effort to satisfy our patients while operating within our values.

Leadership and Management: Our managers' responsibility is to create an environment that promotes an organization-wide commitment to our values, mission, and goals. Effective leadership requires managers to exemplify the behavior that promotes teamwork, motivates productivity, and encourages personal development. Additionally, management provides guidance, consistent support, rewards, and appropriate accountability, which are all essential for our success.

EXHIBIT 2.7	Sample Code of Conduct for Meetings and Interactions

1. **Show Respect and Recognition** —Treat coworkers, customers, and vendors with dignity, empathy, and professionalism.
   - Make eye contact.
   - Avoid negative body language.
   - Be engaged in the conversation.
   - Employ direct communication of issues and concerns with the affected person(s). Do not talk about each other behind their backs.

2. **Value All Opinions and Ideas** — All ideas should be listened to. Remember that the final solution is usually a compilation of previous ideas.

3. **Seek to Understand, Then Be Understood** — Before responding, make sure you understand what you are responding to.

4. **Seek to Understand Constructive Criticism** — Listen to the feedback, and respond professionally. Do not lash back.

5. **Share Information Openly and Provide Your Point of View** — Eliminate "Group Think." Develop thoughts and convictions and contribute them to the team. Synergy comes from building on each other's ideas. The idea is king. If you have a suggestion or are in disagreement, say so with words.

6. **Refrain from Sidebar Conversations** — Do not participate in sidebar conversations, especially regarding a comment someone else in the meeting has just made.

7. **Solve Problems as They Arise** — Use initiative, energy, and creativity to tackle problems head-on. Do not let them fester.
   - Address concerns at the meeting. If this is not possible, address concerns with the individual.
   - Take ownership of a problem you identify and your response to it.

8. **Keep Discreet Information Confidential** — Discreet and confidential information must stay within the management team. No discreet information should leave the room.

9. **Involve Impacted Groups/People in Decision**s — When making decisions, ensure that all impacted decision makers are represented and/or involved. Be aware of them and Include them in the decision-making process early on.

10. **Manage Meetings Effectively** —
    - Stick to the agenda at each meeting. If the agenda is met, bring the meeting to an end.
    - Come to the meetings with deliverables prepared; let the meeting owner know in advance if this will not be possible.
    - For each open issue at a meeting, identify an assignee and a due date to which he/she is willing to commit.
    - Follow through on action items.
    - Summarize decisions made and distribute to all impacted decision makers.

NOTE: This exhibit is also on the CD.

EXHIBIT 2.8	Sample Code of Conduct

- ➤ When there is confusion about whose needs we are meeting, we step back and ensure that we are always putting our patients' needs first.

- ➤ We say only positive comments about our organization to others, and when we point out a problem internally, we try to offer suggestions about possible solutions.

- ➤ We keep sensitive information confidential.

- ➤ To resolve a conflict with someone, we go directly to that person first.

- ➤ We speak positively about others, and when someone complains to us about another person, we send him/her directly to the person involved to solve the issue.

- ➤ When a conflict has reached an impasse, we ask Human Resources or other experts for assistance.

- ➤ When we make commitments, we follow through in a competent, timely, and professional manner.

- ➤ When we make a decision in a meeting, we will not change that decision later without consent from attendees, or we will inform them why the decision had to be changed.

NOTE: This exhibit is also on the CD.

COMMUNICATING THE VISION AND THE MISSION

Some medical practices are now printing their vision and mission on the reverse side of their business cards. It feels quite reinforcing to have your name on one side of the card and the vision and mission on the other. It can make you feel as if you are tied more closely to those broad goals.

Additionally, some organizations have created brochures and other marketing materials that describe the vision, mission, and values. Often, these materials include pictures of what the values mean. For example, one practice showed teamwork as demonstrated by several people working together. Kindness can be shown by one person giving flowers to another. Caring can be depicted with one person wiping a tear from another's face.

Many facilities have framed the vision, mission, and values statements and placed them in very visible positions around the offices.

Patchwork quilts have become popular images that represent the vision, mission, and values. Sometimes each department creates a section of the quilt, and when all the pieces are sewn together, patients and families get a sense that the whole campus works as one to create a quality and caring organization. Some facilities place the large patchwork quilt in the lobby so that everyone — physicians, other team members, patients, and visitors — can see what is important to the people who work there.

IF YOU BUILD IT, THEY WILL COME

Team members also want to contribute to success. A good example of this is a situation that happened with Gisela, a woman from Cuba who worked in housekeeping. One day when I arrived at my health care facility at 8:30 a.m., I was surprised to see Gisela waiting by herself in my office. Gisela always worked the evening shift, so I was concerned by her presence. As I entered, she started speaking with her thick, Cuban accent. "Susan, I know you'll understand, but I wanted to tell you. You always say to give care to our patients. Last night, a woman was in a car accident, came to our ER and needed emergency surgery. She couldn't speak English, only Spanish, and she was crying hysterically. I was supposed to clean all the meeting rooms, but checked the schedule for meetings for today and quickly cleaned only the ones that were needed. Then I sat with the patient for 3 hours to help her feel better until she went to surgery. But I didn't get to finish my cleaning assignment. Is that OK?" Gisela understood what the goals were — and took a risk to meet them.

CREATE A VISION THAT INSPIRES OTHERS

People will live "up to" or "down to" the vision that leaders create. In staff meetings during the building of our new hospital of the future, I frequently spoke about the vision we were creating. One day I said, "We aren't just going to be the flagship of AMI (American Medical International, Inc.), we are going to be the starship!" Because of my upbeat delivery of the message, several on the team smiled and some even laughed. However, on Boss's Day a few months later, I walked into my office to find a huge, laminated, 8-feet-long-by-4-feet-wide banner suspended from the wall behind my desk. The banner said "We are the Starship!" People want to be a part of a vision that raises them to new heights and appeals to their greatness.

Exercise   **Cash on the Spot**

When working with groups of leaders, I often ask them to write down from memory the vision, mission, and values of their facility. Try it. My belief is that these should be on the tip of the tongue of everyone in the facility. See how you and your management team do!

To keep it fresh in everyone's mind, I've been known to walk around a facility, asking people, on the spot, to recite the organization's vision, mission, or values. If they get them correct, I reward them with cash on the spot — sometimes $1, sometimes $5! It's amazing how quickly they equate my visit with the vision and mission.

NOTE: This exercise is also on the CD.

Exercise   **Name that Mission!**

There's a country music song that declares, "If you don't stand for something, you'll fall for anything." When it comes to your practice, what do you stand for? How do you like to be remembered when your team talks about you? What would your team members say that you stand for?

During the past week, name one action you performed that demonstrated your belief in the mission and values? Did anyone see these actions? How did you promote the mission and values? Was it something you said? Something you sent out in an e-mail?

NOTE: This exercise is also on the CD.

THE GOAL OF GOALS

Another component of Box 1 are goals — both long term and short term. In the next chapter, we discuss strategic planning and business planning, which naturally lead to long-term and short-term goals. Short-term goals are manageable, often by fiscal years. For this discussion, long-term goals are those that may be reached after 1 year and often within 1 to 5 years.

What is a goal? A goal is an end toward which you direct specific effort. Where the vision, mission, values, and norms are general intents, goals are specific and measurable accomplishments to be achieved within a specified time and under specific cost constraints.

SMART GOALS

One of the best ways I've found for organizations to be successful is to set SMART goals. These are goals that are specific, measurable, achievable, results-oriented, and time-bound.

Specific means detailed, particular, and focused. A goal is specific when everyone knows exactly what is to be achieved and accomplished. If goals are fuzzy, imprecise, and unquantifiable, you and your team will not know when you've reached the outcome.

Measurable goals are quantifiable and provide a standard for comparison that indicates when the goal has been reached. Doing something "better" or "more efficiently" does not provide the quantifiable measurement necessary to determine goal achievement. "Increase our patient satisfaction score by 10 percent" is a measurable goal.

Achievable means reachable, realistic, and possible. A goal can be a stretch goal as long as it is achievable. If goals are too lofty, we can get discouraged and lose the motivation to be goal oriented. For example, a goal to "eliminate staff absenteeism" is unachievable. A goal to "decrease staff absenteeism to 15 percent" would be more achievable.

Results-oriented means actively focused on an outcome or performance of an operation. SMART goals are action oriented and contain action verbs. Examples of action verbs are *create, increase, develop, produce, complete,* and *improve.*

Time-bound means that there is a deadline for reaching the goal. Without time constraints, people generally put off doing things. It seems that we can always find something else to do that appears to have higher priority. Imposing a deadline motivates us to be goal focused; the deadline must be precise to promote a sense of urgency. In fact, the more specific our deadline, the better chance there is for success. For example, a deadline for completing an assignment by "the spring" or "March 1" can accelerate the need for action.

Three Types of SMART Goals

There are three main types of SMART goals: *essential goals, problem-solving goals,* and *innovative goals.* By understanding these three types, you will find it easier to identify the possible opportunities for setting obtainable goals and achieving desired results.

Essential goals are necessary for continued, ongoing progress. They identify activities needing improvement and are the types of goals that must be accomplished on a routine basis. An example of an essential goal is "By 4 p.m. each day, review list of patient phone calls to ensure that all patients have had their call returned by the end of the day."

Problem-solving goals identify a current problem or opportunity and the desired future situation. These goals pinpoint actions needed to improve performance. An example of a problem-solving goal is "Starting immediately, all insurance forms are to be completed in full and signed by the patient or guardian prior to seeing the physician."

Innovative goals identify ways to improve the current condition. These goals improve good activities by making them better — more efficient, easier, safer, faster, less expensive, or more profitable. An example of an innovative goal is "By January 1, create a two-page, streamlined patient questionnaire that includes patient and family health history plus insurance information."

Performance Goals

Performance goals for the entire organization are generated at the top of the organization, then cascade down through the departments, groups, and individual levels. Each of these goals supports the business strategy of the medical practice. Performance goals are often identified in terms of:

➤ Financial outcomes (for example, revenue, net income);

➤ Operational outcomes (for example, patient satisfaction, quality); and

➤ Behavioral outcomes (for example, performance by physicians, nurses, other team members/application of knowledge).

DASHBOARDS FOR ORGANIZATIONS

Many medical practices are creating dashboards that measure how the practice is doing against the performance goals. When you peer at your car's dashboard, you can quickly assess how the car is functioning and receive timely alerts when something goes awry. Organization dashboards offer something similar — a consolidated view of key information about the goals, including alerts when trouble is looming.

These dashboards are essentially a snapshot of key indicators that provide a way to quickly identify and monitor important factors to ensure that the practice is on track toward its goals. Dashboard gauges can be created based on what's important to your organization. Some broad goals can include the following: quality, financial, patient satisfaction, team member satisfaction, productivity, compliance, continuous improvement/innovation, and growth in market share.

As these broad goal areas are developed into specific measurable categories, key indicators can be developed. For example, the financial goals can include measurement areas such as revenue, accounts receivable (A/R) days, collection percentage, charges on hold, lost charges, overtime costs, and staff productivity.

Just as it would be dangerous to take a coast-to-coast flight on a commercial airliner that had no instrumentation, running your practice without a dashboard could be just as dangerous. When one or more of the key performance indicators underperforms, you can drill down to the root cause and take corrective action.

The organization dashboard can do the following:

- ➤ Identify, track, trend, and correct problems as you evaluate the health of key areas in your organization;
- ➤ Promote more informed decision making and better results;
- ➤ Eliminate duplicate data entry;
- ➤ Continually identify operational efficiencies; and
- ➤ Proactively identify and apply corrective measures.

See Exhibit 2.9 for a sample dashboard of organizational goals.

EXHIBIT 2.9 **Dashboard of Organizational Goals**

Sample Dashboard Goals[4]

Patient Satisfaction:

- Increase patient satisfaction score by 5 percent.
- Decrease average patient wait time to 10 minutes.
- Increase patient retention by 5 percent.
- Increase patient comments/notes by 5 percent.
- Increase patient referrals by 5 percent.
- Follow up patient visit with phone call.

People Commitment:

- Increase retention rate to 85 percent.
- Increase team member satisfaction score by 5 percent.
- Eliminate turnover during first three months.
- Increase recruitment referrals by 5 percent.
- Hold 1:1 coaching sessions monthly for each team member with his/her manager.

Quality:

- Increase accurate prescription dosage by patient.
- Increase score for quality indicators by 5 percent.

Financial:

- Increase net operating revenue by 5 percent.
- Decrease overtime by 5 percent.
- Improve collection rate by 6 percent.
- Decrease A/R over 60 days by 10 percent.
- Increase productivity by 4 percent.

Ethics and Compliance: Complete charts within 24 hours of patient visit.

Innovation and Improvement: Improve three processes per year.

Growth in Market Share:

- Increase physician visits by 5 percent.
- Hire two new physicians this year.
- Send a marketing mailer two times this year.
- Call each patient before visit to reconfirm.

Exercise   **Purposes Critique**

➤ Do we have formal vision, mission, values, and norms?
- What documents concretely define our purposes?
- Do we have SMART goals throughout our organization?

➤ How good is the fit between our stated purposes and patient needs?

➤ To what extent do most people in the organization understand the purposes?

➤ What are examples of behavior that show a strong connection between behavior of the team members and the values and norms that we espouse?

➤ What are examples of behaviors that tend to contradict our formal purposes, showing lack of clarity or lack of agreement?

NOTE: This exercise is also on the CD.

R_x   CHAPTER PRESCRIPTIONS

➤ Define the purposes of your organization so that you can relay them to your team members, enabling all to work together to achieve them. Ensure that your vision is inspiring.

➤ Compose a clear, purposeful, and attainable mission that will help delineate the purpose and goals for your organization.

➤ Clarify the values of the organization in order to emphasize the particulars that set you apart from other organizations. These values will be essential in providing clear and strong leadership to your team.

➤ Develop norms (rules of conduct) to reinforce the values so that behavior of all team members is consistent and supports the purpose.

➤ Set short- and long-term goals that help you achieve and maintain the values, mission, and purposes of your organization.

REFERENCES

[1] P. Senge, *The Fifth Discipline* (New York: Doubleday/Currency, 1990).

[2] J.M. Kouzes and B.Z. Posner, *The Leadership Challenge* (San Francisco: Jossey-Bass, 2003), 87.

[3] C.A. O'Reilly, "Corporations, Culture, and Commitment: Motivation and Social Control in Organizations," *California Management Review* 23 (1989): 9–17.

[4] Q. Studer, *Hardwiring Excellence* (Gulf Breeze, FL: Fire Starter Publishers, 2003), 51.

CHAPTER 3

Strategic Planning ·····································

"**I**f you don't know where you're going, any road will take you there," said the Cheshire Cat in *Alice in Wonderland*. If you're starting out on a road trip, it's imperative that you have a destination in mind. The same is true in organizations. The destination or goal must be clear before a successful strategy can be developed.

So, the first essential step is to develop the organizational goals and then develop the strategy that will align team member performance with those organizational goals. These goals flow from the medical group's strategic plan. Simply put, strategic planning is an ongoing process that determines where the medical group wants to go over the next one to five years, how it's going to get there, and how the group will know that it has arrived.

There are many models and approaches that can be used in a strategic planning process. First, I'm going to focus on the goals-based model that starts with the focus on the medical group's mission, vision, and values. Next, the focus of the plan is on developing goals that will support the mission, then the strategies to achieve the goals, and finally the action planning that delineates who will do what by when. Some plans are for 1 to 5 years, whereas some extend 10 years into the future. Some plans are only five to seven pages long, yet others may be much longer.

Many executives find that the strategic planning process itself is more important than the strategic planning document because during development of the plan, the key stakeholders and senior managers of the medical group clarify where they want the practice to go and how it will get there.

BENEFITS OF STRATEGIC PLANNING

What are the benefits of strategic planning for a medical group practice? Strategic planning serves many purposes for medical groups; for example, it:

➤ Clearly defines the purpose of the medical group and establishes realistic goals consistent with that mission;

➤ Communicates those goals and objectives to the medical group's constituents;

➤ Develops a sense of ownership for the plan, goals, and mission;

➤ Ensures that the most effective use is made of the medical group's resources by focusing the resources on the key priorities;

➤ Provides a baseline from which progress can be measured;

➤ Builds consensus about the vision and direction of the medical group;

➤ Builds a stronger team among the board, executives, and staff;

➤ Provides clearer focus for the medical group, producing more efficiency, effectiveness, and productivity; and

➤ Solves major problems.

CONSIDERATIONS PRIOR TO A FORMAL STRATEGIC PLANNING SESSION

The first step in strategic planning is for stakeholders and senior leaders to look externally and analyze the current situation by studying the health care industry and environment, and then to look internally and analyze the medical group. When I'm conducting strategic planning with an organization, I circulate questions prior to the initial meeting to encourage participants to get involved early on. Some of the questions are included below concerning the health care industry, external environment, and the medical group itself. In order to explore the medical group practice industry, questions include:

➤ What services does the medical group practice provide? Are there other health care services the organization is competing with?

➤ What is the size of the organization relative to others in the area?

➤ How does the medical group compare in terms of market share, sales, revenue, and profitability with other group practices?

➤ How does the medical group compare with others in terms of financial ratio analysis?

➤ What is the medical group's major competition? Who are the major constituents?

➤ What are the trends in terms of government control, political influence, or public atmosphere that could affect the health care industry?

In order to explore the medical group practice environment that encompasses the social, technical, economic, environmental, and political arenas, my questions include:

➤ Are there any trends in the environment (social, technical, economic, environmental, political) that could have a positive or negative effect on the medical group practice or current strategy?

➤ What is the state of the economy? Inflation? Recession? Depression?

➤ What is the cultural, social, and political atmosphere?

The next step is to explore the medical group practice itself, and my questions include:

➤ What is the organization's mission? Is it clearly stated? Attainable?

➤ What are the strengths of the medical group practice? Leadership and managerial expertise? Financial strength? Patient preference?

➤ What are the constraints and weaknesses of the organization? Are there any real or potential sources of dysfunctional conflict in the structure of the organization?

➤ What opportunities and/or potential threats are facing the medical group?

COMPONENTS OF STRATEGIC PLANNING SESSIONS

Following the gathering of ideas and data in response to the questions, the next step is to begin meeting with the stakeholders and senior managers to continue the strategic planning process. Below is a 12-step process that I have used successfully for more than 20 years.

Step 1: Analyze the Environment

Analyze those existing and future conditions in the environment that have an influence on the medical group. The objectives in performing this step are to identify new opportunities for existing and new services and products and to identify major future risks to market position and profit margins. Conditions of primary interest would include economic, competitive, technological, governmental, and market forces.

Step 2: Analyze the Internal Situation of the Medical Group

Analyze the group's balance sheet, operating statements from the past five years, profit and loss reports, capital purchases, human resources indicators, lawsuits, and so forth. Review measures of success.

Step 3: Identify Medical Group Strengths and Weaknesses

After an analysis of conditions in Steps 1 and 2, an orderly review of services, products, markets, processes, personnel, facilities, and certain strengths and weaknesses will emerge. Such resource analysis will not only serve to highlight possible competitive advantages available to the medical group but will also tend to focus on opportunities and risks.

Step 4: Consider Personal Values of Top Management

The aesthetic, social, religious, and personal values of top management and influential stockholders exert a significant influence on strategy. Additionally, the emerging constraints of social responsibility and consumerism are factors to consider. Personal values represent both guides and constraints upon the direction of the business.

Step 5: Refocus on the Vision, Mission, Values, and Norms

Review the vision, mission, values, and norms of the medical group. Reaffirm that they provide the right direction for the medical group.

Step 6: Identify Opportunities and Risks

The medical group should, at this point, be able to identify opportunities in the environment for it to fill a unique niche. These opportunities occur when there are specific needs for services and products that the group is uniquely able to supply because of its resources.

Step 7: Define Services, Products, and Market Scope

This task involves the explicit definition of the future scope of the group's activities. The main idea is to concentrate on a very limited number of carefully defined services, products, and market segments. These segments depend on the analysis resulting from Steps 1 through 6 above. Careful identification of the services, products, and market scope is advantageous because it: (a) reduces the time and complexity of decisions regarding acquisitions, new investments, and other elements of the development plan; and (b) allows the organization to focus on decisions and actions that take advantage of their competitive edge.

Step 8: Define the Competitive Edge

This requires a careful evaluation of unique group skills, position, market advantages, and other competitive factors.

Step 9: Establish Goals, Objectives, and Measure of Performance

Quantitative specifications are required to describe many characteristics of the organization and to provide a clear definition of strategy. Quantitative goals may be established for such parameters as annual rate of growth of revenue, profits, return on investment, market share, number of employees, values of assets, debt, standing in the industry, quality indicators, and so forth.

Step 10: Determine Deployment of Resources

Should resources be applied to growth from within or to acquisitions? In which areas should the medical group focus its resources? Readjusting the application of resources is thus established in a manner similar to the grand-scale shifts of personnel and materials in military conflicts. The senior leaders review professional staff and determine where to allocate human resources and where equipment and supplies need to be deployed in order to meet the goals.

Step 11: Communicate Plan Internally and Externally

Communicate plan internally and externally so everyone involved is clear regarding the goals, objectives, and measures of performance. Included in this step is ensuring that each department knows how the goals of the organization affect the performance of their departments.

Step 12: Develop Action Plans in Each Department

Develop action plans in each department and have managers and team members translate the medical practice goals into their performance and behavior. SMART goals are developed for all team members in the practice. As discussed in chapter 2, SMART goals are specific, measurable, achievable, results-oriented, and time-bound.

TIPS FOR CONVERTING ISSUES AND PROBLEMS TO GOALS

The following are some tips to consider when converting issues and problems into goals: gain consensus on the top three to five issues and prioritize them. Additionally, deal with issues you can do something about and clearly articulate them. It is tempting to ignore current major issues in the interest of pursuing more creative, forward-looking goals. Many organizations fail because they focus too far into the future and do not address immediate issues. Also, when articulating the goals, ensure that all team members understand the objectives and that the goals, when achieved, will address each issue.

APPRECIATIVE INQUIRY MODEL IN STRATEGIC PLANNING

Appreciative Inquiry (AI)[1] is an innovative strengths- and values-based process that focuses on what works in an organization, not on what doesn't. It focuses on imagining possibilities and generating new ways of looking at the world.

There are two premises for AI:

- ➤ **Social Constructionism:** This occurs when we create our reality through our language and in dialog with others.
- ➤ **Positive Outcomes Approach:** To the extent that we create a clear vision of what we desire, we act to make that vision a reality. Instead of asking what problems they are having, positive imagery forces stakeholders, leaders, and team members to ask what is working well around them. This approach is based on the assumption that inquiry about strengths, hopes, values, and dreams is itself transformational.

In strategic planning, AI invites all stakeholders to co-create their preferred future by discovering and valuing the best of the past and existing situation (discovery), envisioning a desired or potential state (dream), dialoguing about the potential state, and co-constructing the future (design and destiny). This 4-D cycle includes:

- **Discovery:** The discovery phase starts with an appreciative interview in which people tell stories of their high points and uncover life-giving experiences in their group, department, or organization.
- **Dream:** The stories from the discovery phase are shared in a dream phase, bringing tremendous energy into the room. Various techniques are used to facilitate dialogue around the stories and reinforce positive thinking. Participants are able to envision the group's greatest potential.
- **Design:** Participants construct and align their ideals, values, structure, and mission in the design phase. They ask what the organization would look like if it were designed to maximize the positive core to realize the vision.
- **Destiny:** In the destiny phase, participants declare their intended actions and actual plans to realize the preferred future. They innovate what will be.

AI can result in substantial improvements in organizational productivity, efficiency, and effectiveness because team members are working to further improve what they already regard as beneficial to the organization. Their motivation can also be substantially improved through this process because it allows them to prevail over the frustrations that bog them down and encourages them to concentrate on what they really want to do — find their real purpose, that is, their vision and mission.

Two Approaches

Two different approaches can be used for strategic planning: problem solving and appreciative inquiry.

Problem Solving	**Appreciative Inquiry**
Define the problem.	Find existing solutions (what works).
Analyze the cause. Fix what's broken.	Envision what might be.
Find solution. Develop action plan.	Determine what should be.
Focus on decay.	Focus on life-giving forces.

The basic assumption in a problem-solving approach is that an organization is a problem to be solved, whereas in AI, the basic assumption is that an organization is a mystery to be embraced.

Possible Questions to Use for Appreciative Inquiry

Think of a situation where your organization was working at its inspired best, working just the way you dreamed it could, or where you were giving your best, and the organization was working at its best. Then ask yourself the following questions:

- Who was involved? What happened?
- What was significant or special about what happened?

➤ What is there about the organization that makes this sort of thing possible? What are the core values? Essential qualities?

➤ What would need to be attended to for these qualities to be characteristic (of the organization) all the time?

THE STRATEGIC PLAN

When should strategic planning be done? The scheduling for the strategic planning process depends on the nature and needs of the organization and its immediate external environment. For example, planning should be carried out frequently in an organization whose products and services are in an industry that is rapidly changing.

Strategic planning should be done:

➤ When an organization is just getting started;

➤ In preparation for a new major venture; for example, when developing a new department, division, major new product or line of products, and so forth;

➤ At least once a year in order to be ready for the coming fiscal year; and

➤ Annually, at which time action plans should be updated.

In addition, during implementation of the plan, the progress of implementation should be reviewed at least on a quarterly basis by the board. The frequency of review depends on the extent of the rate of change in and around the organization. Exhibit 3.1 presents a sample outline of a strategic plan.

EXHIBIT 3.1   **Sample Strategic Plan Outline**

1. Facts about the Organization — External and Internal

2. Trends and Where They Appear to Be Going

3. Stated Role of the Organization (Vision, Mission, Values)

4. Strengths/Weaknesses/Opportunities/Threats of the Medical Group. What There Is to Build on in Achieving Ambitions in the Next 5 to 7 Years

5. Issues to Be Addressed

6. Problems That Must Be Solved in Order to Achieve Mission in the Next 1 to 3 Years

7. Opportunities to Be Seized

8. Alternative Planning Solutions for the Next 1 to 3 Years

9. Recommended Course of Action for the Next 5 to 7 Years: Timing and Action

10. Development of Financial Projections

11. Development of Process to Implement Plan: Budgets, Action Plans, Schedules, Resources Needed

NOTE: This exhibit is also on the CD.

THE BUSINESS PLAN

The business plan is an important part of the process to align the strategic plan with goals and team member performance. A sample business plan outline is provided in Exhibit 3.2.

EXHIBIT 3.2	Sample Business Plan Outline

EXECUTIVE SUMMARY

On one page or less, briefly describe the fundamental elements of the business. This is the most important part of the plan. Describe who the audience is, the present and planned products or services, the unique features of these products or services, what investments are required (that is, time, resources, and money) and the projected rate of return, and the management team.

This summary should be readable, concise, believable, and interesting. The primary function of this section is to whet the reader's appetite to read further.

TABLE OF CONTENTS, ILLUSTRATIONS, AND GRAPHS

The table of contents is a road map of the document that follows. Illustrations and graphs are not necessary but are often useful.

DEFINE PRODUCT OR SERVICE

Spend as much time as necessary on a short, easy-to-read description that will explain your product or services to someone who is not an expert in your area. Cite specific reasons why a customer will want to buy the product/service. Relate the product or service to the mission statement.

Your description should answer these questions:

- What does the product/service do?
- What is the product/service (physical traits, etc.)?
- Who are the customers? Who makes the buying decision, and what is the relationship between buyer and end user?
- What makes this product/service different?
- How complex is the product/service from the user's point of view?
- Can the product/service be tried with little risk? How?
- What are the results of using the product/service? Does it make something faster, better, easier, cheaper?
- Why will the customer buy the product/service?
- What training is required to use the product/service?
- What regulations are relevant to using the product/service (liability, environmental, federal/state tax, etc.)?

(continued)

EXHIBIT 3.2 (continued)	Sample Business Plan Outline

DEFINE AND DESCRIBE YOUR MARKET

This task enables you to determine how much of your product/service you can sell, where you can sell it, at what price, and how to get it to market. Illustrate the total market and your segment of the market.

MANAGEMENT ANALYSIS

Roles in leadership, marketing, and finance are important to any business organization. Analyze the teams' skills and identify any gaps. Prepare an organization chart and define the responsibilities, authorities, and background of each key team member.

QUALITY ASSURANCE AND RELIABILITY PLANS

Describe the quality you plan to attain and how you will maintain and monitor it.

NOTE: This exhibit is also on the CD.

THE FINANCIAL PLAN

A financial plan is an important part of the process to align the strategic plan with goals and team member performance. The components of a sample financial plan outline are provided in Exhibit 3.3.

EXHIBIT 3.3	Sample Financial Plan Outline

FINANCIAL ANALYSIS

The financial analysis section will reveal what your marketing and operational plans will cost. Provide numbers for three to five years of future operations, plus two or three years of past financial reports for an existing company.

Use monthly, quarterly, or annual time frames for:

- Sales (Unit) Volume and Returns: Use number of units to be sold.
- Sales Forecast and Pro Forma Income Statement: Use projected pricing to estimate future sales and expenses. Include:
  - Net sales (unit price times net unit volume, adjusted for collections)
  - Cost of sales (materials, labor, and overhead) — Use detailed bills of materials, price quotes, and time standards.
  - Gross margin (sales less cost of sales)
  - Operating expense (research and development; general and administrative expenses)

(continued)

EXHIBIT 3.3 (continued)	Sample Financial Plan Outline

- Operating profit (loss) (gross margin less operating expenses)
- Miscellaneous income (non-sales sources such as interest earned, consulting fees)
- Net income (loss) before taxes (operating profit or loss plus miscellaneous income)
- Taxes on income
- Net income (loss) (net income before taxes less taxes)

CASH FLOW ANALYSIS

- Beginning cash balance
- Cash receipts
- Cash disbursements
- Net cash from operations
- Sales of stock
- Purchase of assets
- Funds invested
- Short- and long-term debt
- Ending cash balance

NOTE: This exhibit is also on the CD.

THE BALANCE SHEET

A sample balance sheet is also provided (Exhibit 3.4) because it is an important component when aligning the strategic plan with goals and team performance.

PERFORMANCE/FEASIBILITY GRID

As you're prioritizing the actions in your strategic plan, consider allocating resources based on the feasibility and performance they can create (Exhibit 3.5). Resources include money, people, time, materials, energy, knowledge, and so forth.

EXHIBIT 3.4	Sample Balance Sheet Outline

Prepare a pro forma balance sheet for each year in the business plan. This will reflect the asset management and capital investment decisions and should include assets (current and fixed), liabilities, long-term debt, and any stockholder equity. It may be appropriate to include some key financial ratios:

➤ Return on equity (net income divided by total equity)

➤ Current ratio (current assets divided by current liabilities)

➤ Working capital (current assets less current liabilities)

➤ Debt to equity (total liabilities divided by total equity)

OBJECTIVES AND MILESTONES

Break down milestones and objectives into specific tasks and report the time and money to be expended per task plus the expected or actual date of achievement.

APPENDICES

Use appendices for data that are too detailed for the body of the plan but necessary for analysis. These may include product/service specifications, market research results, detailed market planning information, financial analyses, job descriptions, and responsibilities and tasks for team members.

NOTE: This exhibit is also on the CD.

EXHIBIT 3.5	Performance/Feasibility Grid

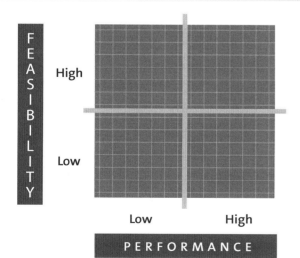

FEASIBILITY: Can be done with current or easily attainable resources, knowledge, and capabilities.

PERFORMANCE: Level of positive impact on goals, key priorities and indicators, and long-term vision for the organization.

Note: As you are prioritizing the actions in your strategic plan, consider allocating resources based on their feasibility and the performance that will occur as a result. Resources include money, people, time, materials.

NOTE: This exhibit is also on the CD.

MONITORING AND EVALUATING YOUR STRATEGIC PLAN

Too many strategic plans end up collecting dust on a shelf. Monitoring and evaluating the implementation of the plan is as important as identifying the strategic issues and goals. After the plan is developed, it's crucial to ensure that your practice is following the steps in the plan.

Strategic plans are guidelines, not rules. So, it's acceptable to deviate from the plan, but it's also important that everyone involved in the planning knows the reasons for the deviations and then updates the plan to reflect the new direction.

Responsibilities for Monitoring and Evaluation

The strategic plan document should specify who is responsible for (1) the overall implementation of the plan, (2) achieving each goal, and (3) monitoring the implementation of the plan. The board of directors usually expects the medical practice manager to regularly report to them about the status of the plan's implementation, including progress toward each of the overall strategic goals. Simultaneously, the practice manager expects regular status reports from department managers regarding the progress in achieving their assigned goals.

Evaluating Plan Implementation

Key questions need to be asked when evaluating implementation of a strategic plan. First, are the goals being achieved? If they are, acknowledge, reward, and communicate the progress. If not, then consider the following questions:

1. Will the goals be achieved according to the timelines in the strategic plan? If not, then why?

2. Should the deadlines for completion be changed? (Be careful about making these changes — know why you're behind schedule before deadlines are changed.)

3. Do team members have adequate resources — money, staff, equipment, training, supplies — to achieve the goals?

4. Are the goals still realistic?

5. Should priorities be shifted to put more focus on achieving the goals?

6. Should the goals be changed? (Again, be careful about making these changes. Find out why you're not achieving the goals before actually changing them.)

7. What can be learned from your monitoring and evaluation in order to improve future strategic planning efforts?

Frequency of Monitoring and Evaluation

Organizations, like medical practices, that are experiencing rapid change from inside and/or outside will want to monitor plan implementation at least on a monthly basis. Boards of directors should see the implementation status at least quarterly. Medical practice managers and the senior team should review the status at least monthly.

Reporting Results

It is important to write down the status of the monitoring and evaluating. Answer the key questions on p. 46 about the specific strategic goals and your progress toward achieving them. Document action that needs to be taken by management for those goals that are off track.

Deviating from the Plan

The strategic plan is not a strict road map that absolutely must be followed. It's all right to deviate from the plan. In fact, most organizations end up changing direction to some degree when there are changes in client needs, government regulations, availability of resources, and so forth. It's important that organizations stay flexible and vigilant so they can be proactive. The most important aspect of deviating from the plan is that you have a strong understanding of what's going on and the reasons why you're deviating from the plan.

Changing the Plan

Develop a procedure for changing the strategic plan. Include

- Why the changes should be made;
- The changes to be made, including changes to goals, responsibilities, and new timelines; and
- Date the new plan and keep old copies of the previous plan.

Celebrating Success

Strategic planning takes a lot of hard work, negotiation, creativity, decision making, and teamwork. When your plan is completed, celebrate your success.

CHAPTER PRESCRIPTIONS

➤ Define goals that are directly in line with achieving and maintaining the organization's vision, mission, and values.

➤ Create strategies to achieve the desired goals, considering your specific organization (environment, employees, etc.).

➤ Develop an action plan that determines the specific ways these goals will become reality: Who needs to do what in order for this to occur? Remember that some goals will be achieved quickly; others may take years.

REFERENCES

1 F.J. Barrett, "Creating Appreciative Learning Cultures," *Organization Dynamics* 24 (1995): 36–49.

CHAPTER 4

What Good Are Goals?......................

Have you ever worked for someone who said, "I'm not sure what I want, but I'll know it when I see it"? I have; and trust me, this type of thinking creates a very frustrating culture. How can your team perform if they don't know where they're going or when they've reached the destination?

After a team creates its vision, mission, values, and norms (these are lofty, broad-spectrum goals), the next step is to actualize these high-level components into SMART (specific, measurable, achievable, results-oriented, and time-bound) long-term and short-term goals.

Other terms for a goal include *ambition, purpose, target, aspiration,* and *end.* Webster defines a goal as an end that one strives to attain. Goals give you a road map to your future, and they provide something to strive for.

A goal is a dream with a deadline. There's a joke about people who don't set deadlines for accomplishing their goals. The joke says they're headed for "Someday Isle" because their life is a series of "Someday I'll do this …" and "Someday I'll do that …"

Why is it important to set goals? Because goals:

➤ Establish direction for ongoing activities;

➤ Identify expected results;

➤ Improve teamwork through a common sense of purpose; and

➤ Heighten performance levels by setting targets to be achieved.

If you or your organization never set goals, how will you know where you're headed? If no goals exist for progress, how will you know how it's doing? If there aren't goals for achievement, how will you know when you're succeeding? Would you get on an airplane if you didn't know where it was going to land?[1]

SMART GOALS

As mentioned in chapter 2, successful organizations create SMART goals. Examples of SMART goals are:

- ➤ "The physician will see patients within 15 minutes of the scheduled appointment time."

- ➤ "We will reach our revenue goal of $1.2 million by July 31."

- ➤ "Our practice adheres to the 'Sunset Rule,' which means all client calls will be answered before the end of the business day on which the client initially contacts us."

- ➤ "We will increase our patient satisfaction score by 10 percent by December 31."

- ➤ "All patients will be called at least 24 hours prior to their appointment to confirm the appointment."

When you set your goals, you'll want to be as specific as possible. Setting goals is a way to focus your attention on what you want in the future. If you're not specific, you and your team will never know where you are going. By setting SMART goals for your team, not only are you asserting, "I know what I want; have confidence in me," but you're also saying, "I believe you are capable of achieving these goals. I have confidence in you!"

SMART goals are action-oriented and involve an activity, a performance, an operation, or something that produces results. Examples of action verbs are shown in Exhibit 4.1.

EXHIBIT 4.1	Examples of Action Verbs		
chart	schedule	perform	bill
appraise	investigate	inform	restrict
evaluate	influence	authorize	create
document	interview	quantify	provide
prepare	increase	identify	monitor
improve	select	research	plan
review	process	identify	implement

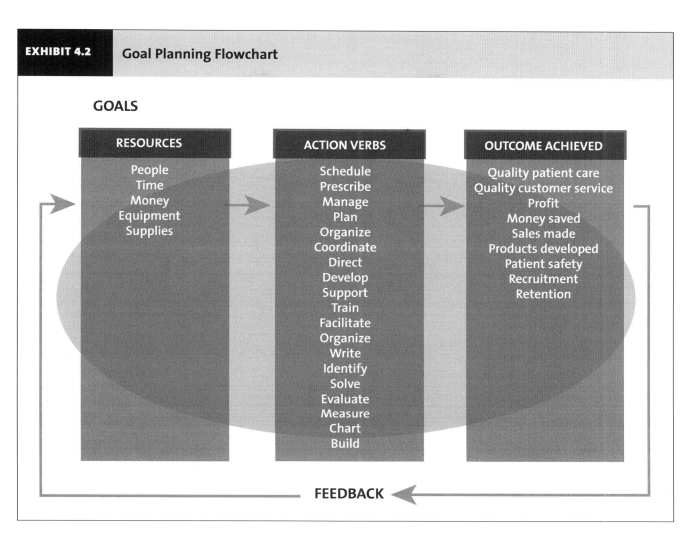

EXHIBIT 4.2 Goal Planning Flowchart

GOALS

RESOURCES	ACTION VERBS	OUTCOME ACHIEVED
People	Schedule	Quality patient care
Time	Prescribe	Quality customer service
Money	Manage	Profit
Equipment	Plan	Money saved
Supplies	Organize	Sales made
	Coordinate	Products developed
	Direct	Patient safety
	Develop	Recruitment
	Support	Retention
	Train	
	Facilitate	
	Organize	
	Write	
	Identify	
	Solve	
	Evaluate	
	Measure	
	Chart	
	Build	

FEEDBACK

As shown above (Exhibit 4.2), goal setting is a dynamic process that includes resources, action verbs, and results in achievements. There is continuous feedback on your progress.

THREE TYPES OF GOALS

There are three types of goals: essential, problem-solving, and innovative. By separating goals into these three types, it is easier to prioritize where to focus your time and energy.

- ➤ Essential goals are required for the operation of the business or for personal improvement. Essential goals must be reached.
- ➤ Problem-solving goals identify a less-than-ideal condition and propose a solution that should be done.
- ➤ Innovative goals are activities that will result in something better, faster, cheaper, easier, or safer. It would be a good choice to reach these goals.

CONTRIBUTING TOWARD A COMMON GOAL

Peter Drucker, a brilliant leadership guru, addressed the importance of having everyone in the organization focused on the overall goals:

Any business enterprise must build a true team and weld individual efforts into a common effort. Each member of the enterprise contributes something different but they must all contribute toward a common goal. Their efforts must all pull in the same direction, and their contributions must fit together to produce a whole — without gaps, without friction, without unnecessary duplication of effort.

Business performance therefore requires that each job be directed toward the objectives of the whole business. And in particular each manager's job must be focused on the success of the whole. The performance that is expected of the manager must be derived from the performance goals of the business; his results must be measured by the contribution they make to the success of the enterprise. The manager must know and understand what the business goals demand of him in terms of performance. And his superior must know what contribution to demand and expect of him — and must judge him accordingly.

If these requirements are not met, managers are misdirected. Their efforts are wasted. Instead of teamwork, there is friction, frustration and conflict.[2]

ALIGNMENT BY SETTING TEAM GOALS

To illustrate the importance of including every team member in the goal-setting loop, I'd like you to think about taking a family vacation. You and your spouse are the family leaders, so the first steps for you to take are that you'll need to agree upon where to go and how to get there. Suppose you agree on the destination, but your spouse would choose to drive the car, and you'd rather fly in order to get there faster. After everyone arrives, you might want to visit all the historical landmarks, but your spouse wants to take a bunch of books along and spend the whole time reading, and your kids want to hit the beach every day. Instead of a nice break, there will be lots of discord, frustration, and broken dreams.

This same type of misalignment can occur in organizations for many reasons, including:

➤ Fuzzy measures and targets;

➤ Unclear strategies and weak top-management commitments;

➤ A gap between organization goals and department goals, or department goals and individual team member goals; and

➤ Failure to connect individual or team accountabilities to rewards.

Research shows that fewer than 20 percent of employees know their organization's business strategy. Only two-thirds of vice presidents believe that their leadership team is in agreement on the business strategy. Consider the impact on employees and on an organization's ability to embed its strategic goals into department goals when less than 20 percent of organizations are fully aligned. Recent research finds that 15 percent to 25 percent of workforce time is wasted on low- or no-value activities.[3]

As discussed in chapter 2, aligning every team member with the vision, mission, values, and goals is critical to success in all organizations, especially medical practices, where the health and wellness of patients is the purpose.

So, how do you start to set SMART goals and cascade them throughout the organization? Start by setting organizational goals for two to five years, and then set SMART short-term goals for one year. The key to successful goal-setting is for everyone on the team to accept and own the goals. When people actively participate in developing their goals, they become motivated to reach the target. The number of meetings depends on the size of your organization. You may need one goal-setting meeting, if you're small. If your organization is larger, you may need several meetings to reach everyone in the organization — one with the practice management, another with each department manager, and then others with team members. I believe it's important to include your part-time team members, too.

The following steps can be followed for setting aligned goals:

Step #1: Review your vision, mission, values, and norms.

Step #2: Review long-term goals and short-term goals for the entire organization.

Step #3: Ask each person to set goals for his/her own area of responsibility.

Step #4: As a team, discuss each team member's goals and determine the degree of fit with the team goals and broader (short- and long-term) goals of the organization.

Step #5: Resolve any differences between the individual and the team, as well as team and organizational goals.

Step #6: Modify team and individual goals based on the discussion.

Step #7: Discuss and establish methods for reaching goals.

Step #8: Identify ways to measure achievement and establish time lines for monitoring progress.

Step #9: Check for understanding of everyone's goals.

Step #10: As a group, establish times when performance will be reviewed.

Step #11: Write down every goal.

WRITE DOWN YOUR GOALS

Several studies have shown that writing down goals increases your chances for success — it encourages you to focus on the goals and achieve success. A study of Harvard alumni 10 years after graduation looked at the correlation between written goals and success. Group A, comprised of 83 percent of the class, had no goals and was making X dollars. Group B, comprised of 14 percent of the class, had unwritten goals and was making three times the income of Group A. Group C, 3 percent of the class, had written goals and was making 10 times the income of Group A.

After the goals are set, progress toward them must be constantly monitored. Don't just mention these goals once in January and expect that people will remember or adhere to them for the rest of the year. A football coach won't exhort the team, "We're going to the Super Bowl!" at the beginning of the season and then drop the topic. The coach repeats this goal over and over again throughout the year to motivate the players. It's important to talk about the goals in meetings and during coaching sessions — visibly show how you're doing in moving toward them in your newsletter by graphing the progress. Then celebrate success as you reach the milestones.

VISUALIZE SUCCESS

The next step is to think positively about the goals and to encourage your team to do so as well. How we think is everything — our thoughts drive our actions. Both our conscious and subconscious minds are critical to success. We become what we think about. Throughout all history, philosophers, historians, and even poets have written about the power of the mind. The Bible proclaims, "If thou canst believe, all things are possible to him that believes." Even 2,500 years ago, Buddha said, "All that we are is the result of what we have thought."

When I'm working with organizations as they set goals, I often quote several famous philosophers from the past century who were convinced of our mind's power. For example, Norman Vincent Peale said, "Change your thoughts and you change your life. If you think in negative thoughts, you will get negative results; if you think in positive terms, you will achieve positive results. In three words, 'believe and succeed.'" William James, the first great modern philosopher of the subconscious said, "The greatest discovery of my generation is that human beings can alter their lives by altering their attitudes of mind. If you wish to be rich, you will be rich. If you wish to be learned, you will be learned. If you wish to be good, you will be good. You must really wish these things and wish these exclusively …" There are two other experts I like to quote. Ralph Waldo Emerson said, "A man is what he thinks about all day long" and "The ancestor of every action is thought." Henry Ford, a visionary leader and inventor, said, "Whether you think you can or think you can't, you're right."

So, people act as they think, and we become what we think about. Our thoughts determine our character, our career, our everyday life. If we think about a concrete goal, we become that goal. If we don't have goals and our thoughts are confused and full of fear and doubt, our life becomes full of confusion, fear, anxiety, and doubt.

I've found *The Magic of Believing* by Claude Bristol to be an excellent resource for understanding the power of our minds.[4] Bristol writes about the importance of both our conscious and subconscious mind in reaching goals — our conscious mind is the source of *thought,* and our subconscious is the source of *power.* Our subconscious works constantly while we're awake and asleep. It can actually fast-forward and see us already being successful! Bristol says that powers of our subconscious include: intuition, emotion, inspiration, imagination, organization, memory, and dynamic energy. Our subconscious assimilates all that is needed for us to reach success — we just need to keep focused on the goal without "letting up," no matter how long it takes, and learn to be patient.

An important point about our subconscious is that it doesn't have a sense of humor — it can't take a joke! Every time our conscious mind says, "I can't do that" or "That's too hard," our subconscious mind says, "You're right!" Every negative thought we have becomes a goal. If we say, "I'll never be promoted," or "I'll never finish college," or "I'll never find love," our subconscious says, "That's right." Effective leaders can maximize the team's performance by encouraging their team to visualize success.

CREATE CASCADING GOALS

Active participation by ALL team members is the surest method for success. When there is open discussion, collaboration, negotiation, and then agreement, you can create ownership and motivation for everyone in the organization. Exhibit 4.3 presents an example of cascading goals.

In Exhibit 4.4, each individual commits to the share s/he is capable of contributing to the overall organizational goals. These goals could involve finance, customer/patient satisfaction, quality, and so forth.

According to Tom Peters, a management guru for 25 years, 80 percent of an organization's projects fail. Businesses spend only 20 percent of their time planning how they are going to execute their projects. Exhibit 4.5 is a planning tool that I frequently use to assist organizations in planning. It's a goal planning document that outlines steps to take when developing SMART goals and involves the whole organization in the process of achieving them.

EXHIBIT 4.3   **Example of Cascading Goals**

GOAL: PATIENT SATISFACTION
       INCREASE PATIENT SATISFACTION SCORES BY 5 PERCENT

The goal of the practice is to increase the patient satisfaction score by 5 percent. Effective leaders will ensure that they communicate this goal to every employee in the practice. Leaders will talk about this goal in every staff meeting and every newsletter, and they will model behaviors that demonstrate that patient satisfaction is important. There will be strategy sessions to talk with every team member about how they can impact patient satisfaction.

Below are some examples of performance goals that could be developed so that every member of the practice can participate in achieving higher patient satisfaction scores.

Physicians

➤ Every morning, physician will call patients from previous day to ensure understanding of prescriptions, treatments, and next steps, and to query if they have additional questions.

➤ During patient visit, physician will sit down next to patient and touch patient at least once during the visit.

➤ After examining patient, they will conclude the visit by asking patient, "What other questions do you have for me?"

Entire Staff

➤ Every six months, each team member will sit in the waiting room for 15 minutes wearing eyeglasses smeared with petroleum jelly (as a means of developing empathy for patients who have cataracts) and cotton in their ears (empathy for those who are hearing impaired).

➤ Each team member will use service recovery skills when dealing with disgruntled patients who are tired of waiting and start to leave the office while angry. "I agree it is a long wait, and I would be frustrated, too. I am very sorry for this delay; let me see how much longer until the doctor can see you." Or "I agree with you and I'm hoping you will stay. I am concerned about you and your [symptoms]. You have already waited this long and I would hate for you to leave and not get the care that you deserve."

Receptionists

➤ Check daily to ensure current, relevant magazines are in the waiting room and patient exam rooms.

➤ When patients have waited 15 minutes, update them on the status of their appointment and apologize. If the wait is more than an hour, give them something "extra" as a part of service recovery (meal voucher, pen and message pad, flowers, health magazine).

➤ Conduct a pre-visit telephone call to verify that the patient remembers the appointment and plans to keep it. It has been shown that this pre-visit call reduces no-shows and tardiness.

© 2009 Susan A. Murphy, MBA, PhD
NOTE: This exhibit is also on the CD.

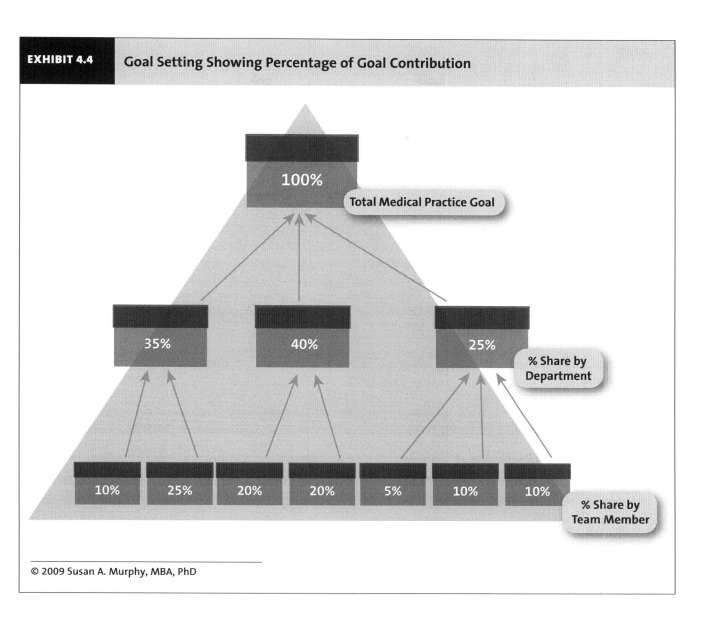

EXHIBIT 4.4 **Goal Setting Showing Percentage of Goal Contribution**

100%

Total Medical Practice Goal

35%   40%   25%

% Share by Department

10% 25% 20% 20% 5% 10% 10%

% Share by Team Member

© 2009 Susan A. Murphy, MBA, PhD

EXHIBIT 4.5	Goal Planning Tool

GOAL PLANNING

GOAL (Specific, Measurable, Achievable, Results-oriented, Time-bound)

_____

_____

_____

_____

BENEFITS FROM ACHIEVING THIS GOAL

_____

_____

_____

POSSIBLE OBSTACLES   POSSIBLE SOLUTIONS

_____   _____

_____   _____

_____   _____

ACTION STEPS	WHO	TARGET DATE	DATE COMPLETED	RESOURCES NEEDED
1. _____	____	____	____	____
2. _____	____	____	____	____
3. _____	____	____	____	____
4. _____	____	____	____	____
5. _____	____	____	____	____
6. _____	____	____	____	____
7. _____	____	____	____	____
8. _____	____	____	____	____
9. _____	____	____	____	____
10. _____	____	____	____	____

IS IT WORTH THE TIME, MONEY, AND EFFORT TO REACH THIS GOAL?   ___YES   ___NO

CHAPTER PRESCRIPTIONS

➤ Set detailed short- and long-term goals that work in conjunction with your vision and mission. Be sure to attach specific deadlines to each goal.

➤ Frequently reflect upon the progress of each goal and create new deadlines if necessary. If a new deadline is set, be sure that you consider why you have to change it, and evaluate the new situation appropriately (learn from the adjustment).

➤ Determine who was responsible for the goal's success or collapse. Praise those who helped make the goal a reality, and talk with those who may have hampered its victory.

REFERENCES

[1] L.A. Rouillard, *Goals and Goal Setting* (Menlo Park, CA: Crisp Publications, 2003).

[2] P.F. Drucker, *The Essential Drucker: The Best of Sixty Years of Peter Drucker's Essential Writings on Management* (New York: HarperCollins, 2003) 112.

[3] W.A. Schiemann, "Aligning People Achieve Top Performance" *Leadership Excellence.* (August 2007): 20.

[4] C.M. Bristol, *The Magic of Believing* (New York: Prentice-Hall, 1948).

CHAPTER 5

Summary ....

Team members are your most valuable asset—when you nurture and grow your team, you nurture and grow your practice. As described in chapter 1, every practice is a dynamic system made up of six subsystems—all of which must be in balance to consistently support the practice goals. If one or more of these subsystems is weak and thus does not support the practice goals, there cannot be maximum performance from the team members.

This first book in the *Maximizing Performance Management Series* is a how-to guide for evaluating the first subsystem, the "purposes." In *Aligning the Team with Practice Goals,* you've learned how to develop the practice's vision, mission, values, norms, and short-term and long-term goals. In addition, you learned that determining the purposes of the practice is essential to developing the practice's strategy. As the Cheshire Cat said in *Alice in Wonderland,* "If you don't know where you're going, any road will take you there." Without a clear purpose and direction, team members become confused, unproductive and less motivated.

Aligning the Team with Practice Goals and the other three books in this comprehensive, results-oriented series provide a road map and prescriptions to take you and your practice to the next level and beyond.

About the Author

∙ ∙

Susan A. Murphy, MBA, PhD, is President of Business Consultants Group, Inc., based in Rancho Mirage, California. Dr. Murphy's extensive professional background combines the worlds of corporate leadership, academia, and management consulting. She has served as an executive in two Fortune 500 Corporations as well as on the graduate faculty at the University of San Francisco. She has also provided international management consulting for 20 years to more than 250 health care organizations and businesses. Clients include Stanford University Department of Pediatrics, Kaiser Permanente, Jet Propulsion Lab (JPL), Tenet Healthcare Corp., the U.S. Air Force, and the Medical Group Management Association.

Passionate about leadership, mentoring, and teaching individuals about gender and generational differences, Dr. Murphy thrives on serving as a catalyst for breakthrough team performance. She has coauthored numerous books including: *In the Company of Women, Conversations on Success, 4genR8tns: Succeeding with Colleagues, Cohorts & Customers,* and *Leading a Multi-Generational Workforce. In the Company of Women,* coauthored with Dr. Pat Heim, has been featured on *Good Morning, America,* the British Broadcasting Corporation, and usatoday.com, as well as in *Time Magazine.* The book was selected as Harvard Business School's "Book of the Month" and has been translated into several languages.

As a keynote speaker, Dr. Murphy is known for her "Wit and Wisdom." Audiences everywhere appreciate her humorous style and useful techniques, as she combines research and theory with real-life experiences. In 2004, Vanderbilt University honored Dr. Murphy with a Lifetime Achievement Award.

Index

Note: *ex* indicates exhibit.

E

Emotional intelligence, assessment of, 10*ex*
Employees. *See* Team members
Empowerment, and alignment of purpose, 16*ex*
Essential goals, 30–31, 51
Executive summary, 42*ex*
Exercises
 on external environment, 12
 on purpose, 29, 34
 on team effectiveness, 9–11*ex*
External forces, 5, 8, 37

F

Fifth Discipline, The (Senge), 19
Financial analysis, 43*ex*
Financial plans, 43, 43–44*ex*
4-D cycle, 39–40

G

Gaffney, John, 4
Gender differences, xviii
Goals, 49–59. *See also* Purpose
 action verbs for, 50*ex*
 alignment of, xiii–xviii, 52–53, xiv*ex*
 assessment of, 9*ex*
 Cascading, 55, 56*ex*
 categories/types of, 17, 30–31, 51
 commitment to, 52
 communication and, 54
 components of, 17, 17*ex*, 29
 dashboards and, 31–33, 32*ex*
 definition of, 29, 49
 importance of, 49
 overview of, 29, 49, 59
 planning tools, 51*ex*, 58*ex*
 "prescription" for, 59
 purposes and, 4
 setting of, 55–58, 57*ex*
 SMART, 30–33, 39, 49, 50, 51

strategic planning and, 35, 38, 39
 visualization of, 54–55
 written, 54

H

Helping mechanisms. *See* Resources

I

Innovative goals, 31, 51
Input/output terms, 7, 8*ex*
Inspiration, 28

J

Jessee, Bill, 22
Johnson & Johnson (J&J), 21
Joint Commission for Accreditation of Health Organizations (JCAHO), 4

K

Kennedy, R.L., 4

L

Leadership
 assessment of, 9*ex*
 business strategy goals and, 53
 importance of, xvi
 input/output terms, 8*ex*
 6 Box model approach and, 2*ex*, 4
 strategic planning and, 36–39, 43*ex*
 values of, 37
 visualization of success and, 54–55
Leading, Coaching, and Mentoring the Team: A How-To Guide for Medical Practices (Murphy), xv
Long-term goals, 17*ex*, 29, 59

M

Magic of Believing, The (Bristol), 55
Management. *See* Leadership

About the CD

· ·

Included with this book is a CD-ROM containing tools, helping mechanisms, and case studies.

HOW TO USE THE FILES ON YOUR CD-ROM

The CD-ROM presents tools and case studies in Microsoft®Word and PDF formats. You can change Microsoft®Word documents, but you can't change PDFs. You must have Microsoft®Word and Adobe® Reader® installed on your hard drive to use the CD-ROM. To adapt any Microsoft®Word file to your own practice, simply follow the instructions below. The CD-ROM will work on Windows and Mac platforms.

Microsoft®Word Instructions for Windows

1. Insert the CD in your CD-ROM drive.
2. Double-click on the "My Computer" icon, and then double click on the CD drive icon.
3. Double-click on the folder named "Maximizing Performance Management."
4. The folders you see are organized into the same categories as those in the book—Tools/Helping Mechanisms and Case Studies. Double click on the appropriate subfolder, and then double click to open the Microsoft®Word or PDF file you wish to download.
5. If you have trouble reading the Microsoft®Word files, click on "View", and then "Normal."
6. To adapt the Microsoft®Word file, you must save it to your hard drive first, renaming it if you like. After you have resaved it, the file can be edited.